THEN COMES BABY

"*Then Comes Baby* is a delightful book for new Catholic parents, full of personal anecdotes and wonderful insights. But most of all, the advice and encouragement you will find is extremely useful in learning how to be the parents God has called you to be. What we like best about this book is that it addresses the new mom and the new dad with equal emphasis. Husbands and wives are together called to build a healthy Catholic family by having a strong faith walk. This book tells them what works when both parents, together, are uniquely aware of the design God intends for families when baby comes."

Dr. William and Martha Sears
Authors of *The Baby Book* and *The Attachment Parenting Book*

"*Then Comes Baby* provides solid, hands-on help and rich Catholic guidance for parents on how to love their child deeply as they strengthen their love for each other. This book will help them become holy families."

Most Reverend Joseph E. Kurtz
Archbishop of Louisville
President of the US Conference of Catholic Bishops

"God wants to fill the hearts of families with the fire of his love. Greg and Lisa Popcak show you how to open to that love through all the joys and challenges of welcoming a new baby. If family life is a gift, *Then Comes Baby* shows you how to unwrap and celebrate that gift in all its forms."

Christopher West
Author of *Fill These Hearts*

"*Then Comes Baby* will help every parent rejoice in both the gift of new life and all the blessings and changes that come with it. The Popcaks articulate a practical vision of family life that is deeply faithful, extravagantly loving, and incredibly joyful. You can create the family your heart desires. This book will show you how."

Damon Owens
Executive Director
Theology of the Body Institute

"Greg and Lisa Popcak remind us that in spite of our fears, God invites us to do the most important work in building a good and holy world: raising children. This wise and practical guide will help parents navigate the sometimes-challenging, often-uplifting work of parenting babies. More importantly, it will remind them to love every minute of it!"

Tim and Sue Muldoon
Authors of *Six Sacred Rules for Families*

Dr. Greg and Lisa Popcak

THEN**COMES**
BABY

The Catholic Guide
to Surviving and Thriving in the
First Three Years of
Parenthood

ave maria press AmP notre dame, indiana

Founded in 1865, Ave Maria Press is a ministry of the United States Province of Holy Cross.

www.avemariapress.com

Paperback: ISBN-13 978-1-59471-411-5

E-book: ISBN-13 978-1-59471-412-2

Cover image © Thinkstock.com.

Cover and text design by Katherine Robinson.

Printed and bound in the United States of America.

Library of Congress Cataloging-in-Publication Data is available.

Contents

Part Four: Hitting Your Stride: Twelve to Twenty-Four Months 189

Part Five: The Year of Wonder: Twenty-Four to Thirty-Six Months 235

Preface

Congratulations! Chances are, if you're reading this book, you either have a new little one on the way or you have recently given birth to or adopted a new baby. As excited as you are, you probably have a lot of questions and a lot of worries. If so, relax! You're perfectly normal, and it's going to be okay. We address many of your biggest questions and concerns in the course of this book.

When we first started our family twenty years ago, we really didn't have a clue what we were doing—even though, between us, we had degrees in education, counseling, and theology. That was all paper. This was real life.

Our Story

Lisa: When we first got married, we weren't even sure we'd be able to have children. I had a serious illness that medication kept under control but that would be fatal to any baby we conceived. When my condition improved three years later, we were so elated! Sadly, our excitement quickly turned to grief when we lost our first pregnancy.

Greg: We really struggled spiritually through that loss, but through it all, God challenged us to draw closer to each other and, more importantly, he challenged much of what we thought we knew about parenting. Up until that point, we hadn't thought that much about parenting. We assumed it would just come to us. I mean, I'm a family therapist. I had good parents. I studied child development in school. How hard could it be?

But we hadn't spent much time considering what it meant to be a Catholic family. After all, we were Catholic, and we were going to have a family. What more could there be to it? We'd raise our kids the way we were raised, take them to Mass, teach them their Catholic prayers, and that would be that. Right?

Lisa: All that is a fine start, of course, but as we discovered, there is so much more for those who are open to learning what the Church has to teach us about the Catholic vision of family life—not just family prayer life, but family life itself. Through the prayer and discernment that resulted from our grief over losing our first child, God showed us that he wanted to give us much more than we had even thought possible. We learned some very hard and some very beautiful lessons by praying through that time. And what we learned enabled us to be more sensitive, more responsive, and more invested in creating the kind of Catholic family we hadn't even imagined when we were first married. God let us know that he had a plan, not just for how he wanted us to pray together, but for how he wanted us to interact with each other and our kids in all situations.

Greg: When God did bless us with children, he gave us the grace to cultivate the kind of love, joy, and intimacy that he desires for every family. I can honestly say that God has taken us by the hand and taught us step-by-step how to build a family with the love that comes from his own heart. The practices we share in this book did not come naturally to us, but the wisdom God has taught us over the years led us to create a much more amazing family than we ever could have if we had followed our original plan. As in all things, God knew better, and in his generosity he blessed us with the most precious treasure possible—an unbelievably close, joyful, faithful family life. We are grateful to have the opportunity to share with you what God has taught us.

Lisa: It hasn't always been easy, and sometimes, like all parents, we wondered if we'd have the strength for what God was asking us to do. But as hard as it's been at times, the fruit has always been worth it. We hope that what you read will be a blessing to you and the family you have started together.

PART ONE

Becoming a Catholic Family

We're guessing that either your Catholic faith is already very important to you or at least you think you might like it to be more important than it has been in the past. Congratulations again! The Holy Spirit often moves powerfully when we experience major shifts in life, and if the birth of a child isn't a major shift, we don't know what is! Whatever your relationship with your Catholic faith was before this new addition, you are probably asking some questions about what it means to be Catholic at this stage of both your life and the life of your family.

The challenges we faced in starting our family and in parenting taught us much of what we know about God's unfailing and unconditional love for us. Through that difficult time, God called us to reflect deeply on how our Catholic faith urged us to think differently about family life than others might. Our children led us to experience God in a deeper and more profound way than we ever thought possible, even though, truth be told, we each had a pretty strong, personal relationship with God to start with. We know we're not the only ones whom God has led on a spiritual journey through parenting.

A good friend of ours, who at one time did not believe in God, realized that he would one day need to answer his child's questions about faith. He recognized that although he had strong feelings on the subject, he didn't have really thoughtful answers. The questions he began asking himself about faith while he and his wife awaited the birth of their first baby eventually led him to become a truly prayerful and deeply engaged Christian. This is not as uncommon as you might think. After all, Isaiah 11:6 reminds us that "a little child [shall] guide them." Sometimes we are willing to change for our children in ways that we would find difficult to change only for ourselves. Many parents are brought to a new level of faith because of the questions that come to mind as they contemplate the new responsibilities they are taking on and the kind of parents they would like to be.

Throughout *Then Comes Baby*, we present the most up-to-date available information on child rearing in a way that encourages your Catholic faith to shine in your heart and your home. Part one offers general tips on getting your family off to a good start and laying the foundation for a great Catholic family. Our Church has an amazing vision for family life, and we want to help you learn how to live that Catholic difference in your home while simultaneously being the best mom and dad you can be. Of course, parenting is a tough job, and it's important to understand how God designed your baby's brain and body to work and how to listen to the messages God has hidden in your son or daughter's makeup so that you can cooperate with God's plan for raising the best, healthiest, most faith-filled, and most enjoyable kid you can. To that end, beginning with chapter 4 we walk you through the changes your baby and family will likely experience from birth to three years. We offer specific guidance about caring for your child, yourselves, your marriage, and the spiritual life of the family at each stage.

CHAPTER ONE

Getting Started

Four Things Every Catholic Family Needs to Know

Certainly [children] are a gift from the Lord,
the fruit of the womb, a reward.
—PSALM 127:3

The first question many new parents ask is "Can we really do this?!?" That's normal. When we were having our first child—and actually each child after—we were both excited and terrified. The excitement and terror were of course greatest when we were expecting our first. Greg was just out of graduate school and in his first job, and Lisa was just overcoming some serious health issues that had caused us to delay starting a family longer than we had expected. We were living in a small apartment and didn't have a lot. Neither of our families was close by. It was as frightening a time as it was wonderful. We asked many of the same questions you are probably asking. How will we manage? How will this change us? Will we like those changes? How can we be sure we're doing it right? Are we really up to this?

The good news is that God loves families, and he wants to teach you how to form a family after his own heart. It doesn't matter what your background is. It doesn't matter where you come from or how healthy or unhealthy your family of origin was. What matters most is that you and your spouse together ask God to teach you what his will is for your family, and then open your hearts to learning all he wants to show you. If you do, you will be able to create a family life that is a blessing both to you and to the people who are privileged to know you. In fact, why don't we start with a prayer asking God to help you do just that!

> Lord, we give you our family. Teach us to love each other as you love us.
>
> Help us to be a family after your own heart. Let us truly enjoy our child as the gift he or she is! Give us the grace to overcome the struggles in our path, the joy to celebrate each little blessing, and the wisdom to live and raise our child(ren) in a manner that gives glory to you. Help us to be inspired by the witness of the Holy Family, and enable us in turn to be witnesses to the holiness you desire for all families. Amen.

Feel free to use this prayer as often as you like, or write a similar one in your own words. Regularly saying a prayer like this together will help you open your hearts to all the wonderful plans God has in store for you and your little miracle.

There are four things we'd like you to keep in mind as you start down the road to becoming a Catholic family:

1. Enjoy your child.
2. God wants to change the world through your family.

3. Marriage and family are the most important activities you can undertake.

4. God wants to show you the way.

Enjoy Your Child

Above all, enjoy your child! Your primary mission as Catholic parents—your most important job—is to discover genuine joy in your life as a family. As Catholics, we know life is a gift. And what do you do when someone gives you a gift? You celebrate—with cake, music, dancing, and laughter! That's what we want your home to be like. That's what Catholic family life is meant to be: a party, with the love and joy you experience in your home as the source of all the things that make life worth living.

We realize that parenting is hard work, just like preparing for a party. If you approach it with the right attitude, all the hard work and exhaustion that comes along with preparing for your feast ends up being just a blip on the radar. You barely remember it. Even while you're working, your focus is almost entirely on how much everyone will enjoy the party and what you can do to make the experience even more wonderful.

We don't mean to imply that family life is easy or that it doesn't take a lot of hard work to have a great family. We understand that some days are going to be a drudgery and some days you're going to be worn out. That's fine. We just mean that you are missing the point if you focus on all the work of parenthood. Sure, you could approach a party thinking, "Ugh, a party. Boo hiss. Too much work. I'd much rather sit here in the dark by myself." But what fun would that be? How much better it is to say, "Ah! These appetizers are going to taste great when they're done! Streamers? Put more over there! Another dessert? Absolutely!"

In our experience, too few parents actually enjoy their kids. They love their kids, but they don't really enjoy them. The world sometimes seems to want us to act like our children are a burden and drag. But Catholics are called to be countercultural, to "make a fuss," as Pope Francis put in his 2013 World Youth Day address, and perhaps the most countercultural thing you can do is parent in a way that enables you to truly know and enjoy your kids.

In all your nervousness, it can be easy to focus on all the work and on "getting it right." But don't worry. You'll be fine. By all means, we hope you will work hard, but we hope you will be able to enjoy every minute of it—or at least most of them. As with the best parties, the more effort you put into your preparations, the more you are able to kick back and enjoy the experience when the guests arrive.

Our children have added so much more joy to our lives than we could ever have imagined or than we could ever say. It's true that we work hard at parenting. In fact, some people tell us that we're crazy to work as hard at it as we do. A lot of people accuse us of making parenting harder than it has to be. But these folks don't understand that the work we do to be present to our children isn't borne out of duty, or obligation, or a sense of dread that we might screw things up, or a compulsion to make up for something in our past. We work hard at parenting because we love a good party! Because life is too short to waste it living in a home with people who barely know each other and rarely relate to each other. We would rather enjoy our kids than not. We would rather hear laughter in our homes than crying and anger. We would rather our home be a place of joy and respite and fun. When we walk in the front door, we would rather feel that we walked into our *home* and not a war zone. Because of the work we put into parenting, our relationship with each of our children truly is a party. It has been since the day they were born. Each one of them is the source of wonderful pleasure.

To be honest, we don't see many families who enjoy their kids or whose kids enjoy them as much as the Popcaks do. We're not bragging. In fact, there is nothing special about us that you can't also have. Not one thing. Our families of origin were fine, but they weren't stellar. Neither of us enjoyed our childhood families as much as we enjoy the family we've created together. Neither of us was born to have this kind of family. God has blessed us by showing us the joy that exists at the heart of the Catholic vision of family life. Actualizing that vision does take work, and as with any work, sometimes you will wonder why you're doing it and what you have gotten yourself into. In those moments, we hope that you will be able to look into the face of your child and see the joy radiating out of him or her because of how comfortable and safe and cared for he or she feels in your arms. And we hope that experience will fill your heart with the kind of joy that makes you delight in the incredible things God is doing in your heart and in your family.

All the suggestions, tips, and best practices we recommend in this book are intended to help you do more than just survive the day with your baby. Sure, there will be days when you feel like that was the best you could do. Again, that's fine. But we want to help you create the kind of family life where at least nine days out of ten you feel gratitude spontaneously bubbling up from your toes for the family you have. That's honestly how we feel about our kids and how parents who put their hearts into our recommendations feel about their kids too. You can't help it. It just happens. Everything that follows in this book is intended to help you experience the kind of joy that most families just don't seem to have. God wants more for you. Your Church wants more for you. We want more for you. We hope you will join us in welcoming the incredible gift God has given you by doing the work that makes your home a celebration of everything that family life can be. We pray that you are willing to invest the time and energy in a family life that enables you to truly know, love, and celebrate the gift you have been given in your child or children.

The first and perhaps most important thing to take away from this book is to *relax*! Don't be afraid to enjoy your kids,

and don't let anyone else talk you out of it—especially the
critical voice inside your head.

God Wants to Change the World through Your Family

Have you noticed that the world is in a bit of a mess? In fact,
for that very reason, many adults think that having children
is irresponsible. They say things like, "I would *never* want to
bring a child into a world like this!"

Catholics view things a little differently. We believe that
children are a sign of God's desire to give us a brighter future.
Pope John Paul II—now St. John Paul II— once said, "A child
conceived is always an invitation to live and to hope."[1] In his
2013 *World Youth Day Welcome Address*, Pope Francis seemed
to concur:

> [Children] are the window through which the
> future enters the world. . . . Our generation will
> show that it can rise to the promise found in
> each young person when we know how to give
> them space. This means that we have to create
> the material and spiritual conditions for their
> full development; to give them a solid basis on
> which to build their lives; to guarantee their
> safety and their education to be everything they
> can be; to pass on to them lasting values that
> make life worth living; to give them a transcen-
> dent horizon for their thirst for authentic hap-
> piness and their creativity for the good; to give
> them the legacy of a world worthy of human
> life; and to awaken in them their greatest poten-
> tial as builders of their own destiny, sharing
> responsibility for the future of everyone.[2]

The world needs families like yours: courageous moms
and dads who are willing to stand up to all the scariness in

the world and say, "See our child? Look at our family. Join us in hoping for a better, brighter tomorrow!"

As excited as you are that you are becoming a family, the Church tells us that God is even more excited because he would like to communicate with the world through you. In fact, he wants to change the world through your family. The work you do as a parent is much bigger than just you and your family. The joy you cultivate in your home will warm your hearts, but even without your intending it, it will also make a difference in the world around you.

> **Lisa:** Because we travel a lot for talks and we always bring our kids with us, we're often at restaurants. I can't tell you the number of times that, even when our kids were tiny, we would have people just randomly come up to us and tell us how nice it was to see a family that enjoyed each other's company, who seemed to be genuinely happy to be together. It never fails to surprise us because we're really not trying to put on a show. We're way too lazy for that. Honestly, it's a little embarrassing. But over the years, it's been driven home to us that people are starving to know it's possible to have a loving, joy-filled family. It can be humbling, but we're happy that people who see our family seem to feel that the warmth God has kindled in our home is contagious.

The Church teaches that every family is called to witness to how—and how much—God loves *all* of his children: generously and joyfully. God wants to show the world that this kind of love is absolutely possible. That's why he inspired you to have a child. Every time you commit yourselves to loving each other generously and joyfully, you are fulfilling the vocation of family life. A *vocation* is simply the way Christians show God's love in the world and for the world. Families do this in a unique and tremendously important way just by being themselves and remembering to love one another while they go about the tasks of everyday life. In the words of Pope Francis, "Christian families are missionary families . . . also in everyday life, in their doing everyday things, as they bring to everything the salt and the leaven of faith!"[3]

The idea that God has big plans for your family can seem intimidating, but the very good news is that you don't have to be perfect for God's will to be done. There will be many days when you argue with each other, get scared together, wear each other out, frustrate each other, and otherwise wonder what you were thinking when you first started this journey of building your family. You are only human, after all. That's actually a very good thing, because God wants to show the world that ordinary families like yours are capable of an extraordinary love through his grace. No matter what you go through as a family, and regardless of whether those challenges are from outside pressures or internal struggles, as long as you always recommit yourselves through prayer to loving each other generously and joyfully through it all, we promise that God will enable you to create the truly close, peaceful, loving family you always dreamed of having. It doesn't matter whether you have the faintest idea what you are doing. God will use the love that shines out of your home through all the ups and downs as a way of drawing the world a little closer to him through you. Just wait and see.

Marriage and Family Are the Most Important Activities You Can Undertake

A lot of people make the mistake of thinking that a family is something you *have* instead of something you *do*. We like to say that *family* is a verb. Too many people think that family just happens when children arrive, but that's not the way family works at all. And it's definitely not how a Catholic family that tries to live and breathe our Catholic faith comes into being. Pope Francis spoke to this exact point in his Holy Mass for the

Family Day homily on October 27, 2013: "We all know that families, especially young families, are often "racing" from one place to another, with lots to do."[4]

This racing character of contemporary family life tends to lead to families that look more like collections of individuals living under the same roof: a group of people always running in a million different directions doing some fairly interesting things but never really relating to each other in any meaningful way. Maybe you are familiar with families that look like this. Maybe your family of origin looked like this. But this is *not* the Catholic vision of family life.

In *The Gospel of Life*, John Paul II said that moms and dads play an important role in evangelizing the world by creating family relationships that witness to "respect for others, a sense of justice, cordial openness, dialogue, generous service, solidarity and all the other values which help people to live life as a gift."[5]

This kind of family life doesn't just happen. You have to work at it. That's why we say that *family* is a verb and why family life is the most important activity you can ever undertake. Especially now that you have been blessed with a child, it is very important that you look at the way you spend your time. Do you plan your work schedule, your activities, and your priorities by thinking *first* of how much time your family needs to cultivate the kind of closeness described in *The Gospel of Life*?

> **Greg:** When we had our first child, I remember thinking really hard about the way I worked and spent my time. I was working a full-time job at the same time I was trying to get my private practice off the ground. It was a lot of pressure, but I knew that I couldn't just focus on my work. I had to remember I was a dad first.
>
> I tried to be careful not to schedule meetings late in the day. I sought to make sure that the last hour or so of my workday was spent doing

paperwork instead of meeting with people so that I could be sure to be available to help Lisa and get some time with our new baby.

In addition to my professional work, I was also the music director in our parish and was involved in community theater. I remember talking over all these commitments with Lisa. We decided together that while my work with the Church could continue, it was important for me to scale back my community theater involvement. The practice schedule was just too much for a new dad. Lisa really appreciated my willingness to let that go, and for my part, I was happy to do it. I'm a ham, and I love acting, but I love her and my family more. I knew that having the kind of family I wanted to have would require me to be present. I didn't merely feel obliged to take a break from my acting hobby; I felt like I had something better to do with my time. Lisa still shares with me how much it meant to her that I chose time with her and the baby over time with my friends at the theater.

There are simple habits you can cultivate to make sure you give your family the best of you. We show you ways to do this better throughout the book, but we want to state right up front that Catholics view family life itself as the most important activity in your week. One of the ways you can let your Catholic faith shine in your growing family is by remembering to prioritize your family relationships. For the Catholic parent, taking time together isn't just a *nice* thing to do—it is the *most important* thing you can do.

Maybe it's important that we stop a moment here. It would be easy to turn this into some kind of penitential lecture about your "duty" to your kids and how to be Catholic you have to "make sacrifices," blah, blah, blah. That's not where we're going with this, so if your head is going there, we kindly ask you to step outside, take a deep cleansing breath, clear your head, and then come back.

Okay? You back?

Terrific! Now let us explain where we are going with this. Of course it can be hard to give up certain things you enjoy. But in the first place, there's no reason to give them up if you can do them and still be present to your spouse and kids. Why make things harder than they have to be? That said, if you do choose to give something up so that you can be more present to your family, don't think of it as letting something go. Think of it as choosing something that much more awesome.

Scripture tells the very human story of what most of us would do if we found some treasure we hadn't dreamed of discovering:

> The kingdom of heaven is like treasure buried
> in a field, which a person finds and hides again,
> and out of joy goes and sells all that he has and
> buys that field. Again, the kingdom of heaven is
> like a merchant searching for fine pearls. When
> he finds a pearl of great price, he goes and sells
> all that he has and buys it. (Mt 13:44–46)

Did the man who gave up all he had to buy the land with the buried treasure resent his "sacrifice"? Did the merchant feel deprived because he had to sell the rest of his inventory to be able to buy the "pearl of great price"? Of course not. What would you be willing to give up if it enabled you to really enjoy being with your kids? We mean *truly* enjoy your kids and take *genuine* delight in your family. What would that be worth to you? What would you be willing to "sacrifice" to be able to create the kind of family that energized you as soon as you walked in the door after work? And not that you're doing this for anyone else, but what would you let go of if it meant having the kind of family that made your extended family and even strangers wonder, "Why are they so happy together? What's their secret?"

Would giving something up to have that kind of family seem like a sacrifice? That's what we thought. And that's exactly the kind of family the Church wants you to have and can teach you to have if you are willing to do a little work. If you make this your reality, you'll be on the way to creating the kind of family that makes God smile. Remember, family life is a vocation; it is the primary way you will bear witness to God's love in the world and for the world. There is no more important way to spend your time. Nothing can come as close to filling your heart with joy as the sense of overwhelming gratitude that comes from having a great family life. It truly is that pearl of great price that will make you happy to give up everything else to acquire it.

God Wants to Show You the Way

Even if you came from a great family, creating your own great family is another matter altogether. For Catholics, it's an even bigger challenge because God doesn't just want you to replicate in your home what your parents did or what you read in some book (even this one). God wants your family to love each other with the love that comes from his own heart. He wants you to experience all the graces, benefits, and joys that come from living family life as he intended it to be lived. So how do you figure that out? Easy. You ask God to show you how it's done.

In his book *Mere Christianity*, C. S. Lewis wrote, "We love . . . because God loves . . . and holds our hand while we do it."[6] What does "holding God's hand" look like? What does it mean? It means taking seriously your commitment to pray together and participate in the sacraments. Lots of Catholics go to church or say various prayers, but it is easy to do these things mindlessly and simply out of habit. Doing these things in this thoughtless way is more like waving at God from across the parking lot than like holding his hand while he teaches us to love. In order to get what God wants to give us from our prayer and sacramental life, we have to prioritize them and try to give our best attention to them. That can be hard to do with a new baby, especially if you haven't done it before (or even if you have). As we accompany you through the first few years of your life as a family, we offer some great ideas for getting the most out of your spiritual life and learning what God wants to teach you. For now, suffice it to say that God gives new parents a million opportunities to hear his voice and know his will for their families.

> **Lisa:** When we had our first baby, I remember being so overwhelmed by all the conflicting parenting advice out there. I didn't have the best family life growing up. My dad died when I was little, and my mom had to work very long hours to keep us afloat. I spent a lot of time on my own. Plus, my mom wasn't particularly religious. In fact, she was the opposite of religious and was pretty antagonistic toward Catholicism in particular. I really didn't have a great sense of what it was to have a close family, much less a joyful and faithful one. I don't mean to say that my childhood was awful—far from it. It just kind of "was," if you know what I mean. I knew I wanted to give our children a better family life than I had, but I didn't know where to start, and it felt intimidating. So Greg and I prayed.
>
> Being new parents, we didn't have much time to sit and meditate. It was hard enough to get through Mass with a baby, much less really pay attention! I remember just trying to pray through all the things I did as a new mom. When I was nursing our baby, I would imagine the Blessed Mother nursing Jesus, and I would ask her to pray for me so that I could have her gentle, loving heart. When the baby would smile or do something that made me happy, I would

thank God out loud for this incredible gift, and I would ask him to teach me how to raise the child he gave us. Our first was a terrible sleeper, and in the middle of the night when I was trying to comfort him, I would pray as much of a Rosary as I could manage as a way of soothing both him and me. Honestly, if it hadn't been for those Hail Marys I'm sure I would have cracked up some nights. Sometimes, when I was really exhausted, I would try to imagine Jesus on the cross loving me, and I would ask him to fill me up with his love so that I wouldn't run out. I don't know how it worked, but it did.

Greg: I remember looking at Lisa nursing our son and asking St. Joseph to teach me to take care of them the way he took care of Mary and Jesus. I had a good dad. He was a faithful and gentle man. But he wasn't nearly as present as I wanted to be, so I asked God to show me how to be there more for my kids. When I was at work, I would take whatever chance I could to pray for Lisa and our baby: that they would be getting the rest they needed, that they would have a good day, and that I could save enough energy so that I could be "on" for them when I finally got off work. That wasn't easy, especially in the early years when I was working two— and sometimes three—jobs to make ends meet. But through it all, the thing I remember most is the light in each of our babies' eyes. I would hold our baby and just look at the joy—the light—and I would pray that God would never let me do anything to make that light go out. It was just so precious.

Sometimes, when I felt tired or resentful or lonely because Lisa was out just when the baby finally fell asleep and she couldn't spend time with me, instead of just surfing the Internet or watching

television, I'd take time to talk to God about what
I was feeling and ask him for the grace to be the
man he wanted me to be for my wife, my baby, and
myself. I'm not very generous by nature. On my own,
I can be pretty selfish. I like what I like the way I
like it, just as anyone else does, I suppose. But God
led me out of that self-centeredness step-by-step
(yes, sometimes kicking and screaming a little bit
too) through those prayer times. It made all the difference in the world. I'm a better man because of
the way God has encouraged me to respond to the
children he has given us.

One surprising source of parenting inspiration has been
the Church herself. We call the Church our "mother" for a
reason. *The Church is literally the Family of God,* and although
many of us don't think about it, the Church parents us through
the sacraments and asks families to follow her example. For
instance, the Mass reminds us that God, our heavenly Father,
takes time out of the busiest schedule in the universe to have
the ultimate family meal with his children each time we celebrate the Eucharist. It's a great reminder of how important
family life is to the heart of God—so important, in fact, that he
modeled the Church after the family. He is our father. By the
waters of Baptism, we are born into new life in Christ through
the Church's womb, the baptismal font. We are nourished at
his table, and he is always present for our family meal.

When we sin against God or our brothers and sisters, our
heavenly Father asks us to spend some time with him—to sit in
the lap of our mother, the Church; tell him what we have done;
and receive the help we need to not do it again. He demands
perfection from us, but he is an incredibly gentle disciplinarian.
Through the Anointing of the Sick, he sits up with us when
we're ill. No matter what we need, he is always there for us
in ways we can see and taste and touch. In a million different ways, the Church reminds us how available God makes

himself to us, providing both quality and quantity time. The Church stands as a spiritual and physical reminder of everything our families are called to be, which is why theologians refer to the family as the *domestic church.*

As we discuss in chapter 15, sometimes parents struggle to get anything out of attending Mass with a new baby or to make time for the sacraments because of the distractions of family life. But even when we leave church not intellectually stimulated or when we walk out more frustrated than when we entered because of our child's behavior, God is still giving us the grace we need to model our family after his—messy, loud, and imperfect, but still beautiful, precious, and holy. We can take comfort in knowing that if God's family is still a work in progress, maybe it's okay that ours is too.

As you start your new life as a family, keep these four things in mind: (1) the best and most important thing you can do is enjoy your little one with all your heart; (2) God has a plan for your family; (3) because of that plan it's important that you intentionally prioritize your marriage and family life; and (4) we don't have to stress out, because God wants to hold our hands and walk us, step-by-step, through learning how to live his vision of family life. Any Catholic family, no matter the background or present skill of the parents, can become everything it was meant to be—everything you dream of for your family.

CHAPTER TWO

Laying the Foundation

Healthy Baby, Healthy Parents, Healthy Marriage

When you are welcoming your first baby, there are two major topics that generate a lot of concern and threaten the fun of becoming a family: negotiating all the conflicting parenting advice and figuring out exactly how to take care of yourselves and your marriage while taking care of your baby.

Many parents feel overwhelmed by the divergent parenting advice. Breast or bottle? Where should the baby sleep? Can we spoil the child by holding him too much? It is hard to find reasonable responses to these questions, much less consensus. Similarly, there are plenty of conflicting recommendations to be found regarding the best ways to take care of yourself and your marriage when a new baby comes on the scene. How do new parents—and especially new moms—find the time they need to rest, to be intellectually stimulated, to maintain romance, and to feel like self-possessed adults, not just parents?

Throughout the book, we offer many specific practical tips to help you make the best decisions for your family regarding these questions (and more) at every stage of your baby's development from birth to age three. Right now, we want to lay out some general principles that could both inform the many parenting decisions you will make and guide you in nurturing yourselves and your marriage over the next few months and years. We want to help you figure out how to parent in a way celebrates the Church's vision of a joy-filled family life. Ready? Let's get to it!

Secular Parenting Principles

Secular parenting advice tends to split into two general camps: *baby-centered* and *parent-centered*. Both approaches have their advantages and disadvantages. As you start down the path to becoming a joyful Catholic family, we'd like to help you sort out the differences and find a way to incorporate the best of both approaches into your parenting style. To do that, we briefly look at each parenting camp separately and then propose a third way forward that draws from the wisdom of our Catholic faith.

Baby-centered advice tends to focus on the importance of "attachment," which has to do with meeting the child's needs promptly and consistently so that the baby's social brain can develop to its fullest capacity. This parenting attitude tends to assume that if the baby is well cared for, then Mom, Dad, and the marriage will work themselves out in time.

Parent-centered advice, by contrast, tends to operate under an opposing set of assumptions: that babies are resilient and bounce back from just about anything and that as long as Mom and Dad are happy and the marriage is strong, the kids will be all right too.

As we previously mentioned, neither approach is completely adequate. Even so, parenting experts and parents have spent a lot of time fighting among themselves about which approach is the right one. Often, those arguments have far less to do with solid evidence from the social sciences than they have to do with philosophy, opinion, the feelings a person has about the way he or she was raised, the importance a person places on his or her own needs, and advice or pressure from a person's parents or in-laws. The lack of serious information to help parents make truly educated decisions has led to the viciousness of the so-called "Mommy Wars" that have been waged for years in print, on the Internet, and in "support" groups (which are often not as supportive as they are competitive).

Fortunately, since the 1990s science has been able to weigh in on the debate and offer parents some concrete information to help them make the best decisions for their families. As it turns out, there is something to be said for both approaches. We look at the advantages and limitations of both secular approaches and then propose a third way, guided by our Catholic faith, which helps us combine the best of each.

Advantages of Baby-Centered Approaches

A vast body of virtually conclusive research—not only from psychology but from brain science as well—now shows that baby-centered approaches such as breast-feeding, nursing on request, room sharing (and bed sharing), prompt responses to infant cries, and high levels of both physical affection and parent-child interaction really do produce the most favorable outcomes as far as the baby's brain development, relational development, and even moral development are concerned. The parenting practices encouraged by baby-centered approaches have been shown by dozens of studies over the last twenty years to foster the growth of the neurological structures that, together, are referred to as the *social brain*.[1] The baby-centered parenting practices previously mentioned have been shown to be directly responsible for helping children achieve the highest level of development in all eight skills associated with a well-developed social brain:

1. *Body regulation:* the ability to keep the organs of the body and the autonomic nervous system (e.g., heart rate,

respiration, body temperature) coordinated and balanced under stress

2. *Attuned communication:* the ability to pick up on the meaning of subtle, nonverbal, physical cues (facial expressions, tones of voice, posture) that indicate another person's emotional states and degree of well-being. Also known as "attunement."

3. *Emotional balance:* the ability to be both emotionally stimulated enough to be aware and engaged in my environment but not so overstimulated that I am easily flooded by my feelings and carried away by them

4. *Response flexibility:* the ability to pause before acting on my impulses and willfully change the direction of my actions if doing so suits me better than my initial impulses

5. *Fear modulation:* the ability to resist anxiety. People with poor fear modulation become easily flooded with anxiety where others might just experience nervousness or even excitement.

6. *Insight:* the ability to reflect on my life experiences in a way that links my past, present, and future in a coherent, cohesive, and compassionate manner. Insight helps me make sense of both past and present experiences.

7. *Empathy:* the ability to have insight (as defined above) into other people. Empathy is the ability to imagine what it is like to be another person and to reflect on their experiences in a way that links their past, present, and future in a coherent, cohesive, and compassionate manner. Empathy helps me make sense of other people's lives, the way they think, and their feelings.

8. *Moral reasoning:* the ability to imagine, reason, and behave from the perspective of the greater good. This includes the ability to delay gratification and find ways to get my needs met while understanding and accommodating the needs of others. [2]

It seems to us that most parents are deeply concerned with fostering all of these traits in their children, because all of these traits have to do with self-control, compassion, and morality. This is not to say that children parented using less baby-centered approaches will not develop these qualities. But research strongly suggests that children reared by more baby-centered approaches are *more* likely to have a better developed capacity for these skills than are children raised with other methods.[3]

But as great as baby-centered approaches are for Baby, how are the parents' needs met? How do you focus so much on meeting Baby's needs and have any kind of energy left for your marriage or personal life? That's where parent-centered approaches bring something to the party.

Important Contributions from Parent-Centered Approaches

After reading the previous observations, you might be inclined to wonder if there is anything good left to say about parent-centered approaches. There is, of course! Two things stand out in particular. First, if parents allow themselves to become burned out by doing baby-centered parenting, it doesn't work nearly as well.[4] Babies—and really, most people—seem to be wired to be more sensitive to *how* things are done than to *whether* they are done. If a parent neglects self-care to the point that he or she feels fried, frustrated, and fed up with parenting or with the child, the benefit to the social brain of baby-centered approaches is actually *less* than if the parent employed more conventional parenting practices such as bottle-feeding and crib sleeping *and* was able to interact with the child more contentedly. This seems to have to do with the amount of eye contact and animation the parent expresses toward the child.

You can do all the "right things" associated with baby-centered practices, but if your heart isn't in them, if you are just doing them because some expert told you that you should in order to be a good parent, then that disconnection shows on your face and in your interactions with your child. The baby senses the disconnection and becomes distressed, and his or her brain locks down. Dr. Ed Tronick's famous "still face experiment" dramatically illustrates this dynamic. A video demonstrating this experiment shows a baby moving from animated and bubbly to stressed and depressed in less than minutes because of his mother's out-of-synch facial expressions.

The second piece of useful information that comes out of research on the parent-centered approach is that babies do best in homes where Mom and Dad's relationship is strong and secure.[5] This is *not* the same thing as saying that as long as Mom and Dad are happy, Baby will be happy too. There is actually a good amount of evidence to show that if Baby's needs are not consistently and generously met, Baby will *not* be well-adjusted no matter how content Mom and Dad are.[6] You can't just focus on your marriage and assume that the kids will be all right because they got to bask in your love for each other as husband and wife. Unhappy marriages *do* negatively affect infant attachment, but happy marriages *don't* positively affect attachment unless the child's needs are also consistently met. That said, parenting is hard work, and the parent or couple who becomes so hyperfocused on meeting Baby's needs that they push themselves or their marriage to the breaking point are not doing anyone—including their child—any favors.

Parenting with the Common Good in Mind

The Catholic Church provides guidance for families on finding the balance between these two approaches in the form of the principle of the common good. The principle of the common good teaches us that those who have the least ability to meet their own needs (e.g., Baby) have a right to have their needs met first. The principle of the common good also states that all people (including Mom and Dad) have a right to get their own needs met, as long as they do it in a way that is respectful to everyone else. Practically speaking, we would argue that this means that parents should challenge themselves on a regular basis to be as baby-centered as possible while being creative about how to meet their own needs. Because responding to Baby's needs promptly, consistently, and even extravagantly has been shown by science to be truly best for Baby and for parents (by making the job of parenting easier and more enjoyable), parents should do what they can to be as fully present to Baby as possible, especially because he cannot meet his own needs. This kind of heroic generosity is called *self-donation* (using everything we have to work for the good of others) and it is a highly valued virtue for Catholics. Self-donation, the Church tells us, is the secret to becoming the joy-filled, loving people God means us to be. As the Church puts it in *Gaudium et Spes*, we "cannot find [ourselves] except through a sincere gift of [ourselves]."[7]

The Church also recognizes that everyone has limits and that those limits must be respected even as they are being gently challenged. Pope John Paul II's theology of the body reminds us that we are not purely spiritual creatures capable of doing all things without experiencing limitations or breakdowns. We are bodily beings who must work within and acknowledge both the blessings and the limitations of our bodies.[8] Saying that we "should" be capable of more is irrelevant if we are not actually, *physically*, capable of more without jeopardizing our health and well-being. If our need for sleep, or nourishment, or intimate connection with our spouse is being not just tested—as parenting tends to do—but stretched to its breaking point, that's not good for Mom, Dad, *or* Baby. That's why parents need to constantly seek creative ways to get time for themselves and their marriage. Taking regular, small actions to care for yourself and your relationship (e.g., napping when Baby naps, making sure to find time every day to talk and pray as a couple) will prevent you from having to take larger, more disruptive actions (e.g., an entire day for me-time or a weekend away with your spouse) to put your mental, physical, and relational health back in order. This creative balancing act is what living out the principle of the common good means in family life, and it is the key to creating an enjoyable family life where everyone's needs are met, including yours.

Pursuing the common good prevents Catholics from saying either baby-centered or parent-centered approaches are the only way to go about things. Rather, pursuing the common good requires Catholic parents to be both sensitive to Baby's immediate needs and creative about meeting everyone's needs in a manner that doesn't shortchange Baby but doesn't totally drain the adults. This takes sensitivity, prayer, communication, and commitment on the part of both parents. We walk you through the steps of this dance in future chapters, but we wanted to set out the goal early on so that you can keep it in mind as you lay the foundation for a healthy, enjoyable, Catholic family life that reflects both generous, self-donative love for your child and good stewardship of your health and the health of your marriage.

Your ability to care for your personal, marital, and family well-being depends on your awareness of the importance of regular routines and rituals in sustaining a happy, healthy home. We look at some of these in the next chapter.

CHAPTER THREE

Routines and Rituals

The Secret to Keeping a Joyful Balance

The key to maintaining joy and a sense of well-being in your personal and marital life now that you have a baby is to protect some degree of routine and ritual in your growing family.[1] That probably sounds crazy. After all, your baby has most likely thrown you completely off whatever normal schedules you may have had. That's to be expected, and to some degree, we all just have to accept and adjust.

Even so, there are some routines and rituals that are important to keep—or institute if you haven't done so already— because they can help you become a parenting "master" rather than a well-meaning but completely done-in "disaster." We give you specific suggestions for healthy and fun routines and rituals throughout the book, but we wanted to get you thinking about these activities now so that you can begin to generate your own ideas as well as checking out our suggestions.

Routines and Rituals: What's the Difference?

Routines and rituals are both regularly occurring, expected patterns of doing things that enable you to have a sense of peace, order, sanity, and enjoyment in your life. They are certain activities you do—no matter what—that help you enjoy the company of your spouse and baby despite the chaos that surrounds you.

Routines have to do with how you manage your day: when you get up, how you get ready, when you have meals, when you pay bills, when and how you clean house, and when you go to bed. Having a baby usually disrupts your familiar routines beyond all recognition, but that doesn't mean that you shouldn't try your best to create new ones. Routines make parenting easier and more pleasant by getting everyone—including Baby—on the same page. Even your baby will intuitively come to know that "First Mommy does X with me and then Y and then Z," which gives your baby a sense of security and calmness that will in turn give you a greater peace of mind.

By comparison, *rituals* are the regularly occurring activities that make your day or week a little special, or more joyful, or meaningful, or on some days, merely bearable. They represent the little moments you reliably take as individuals or together for work, play, talk, and prayer. They bring some measure of comfort, continuity, and confidence.

Think for a moment of the golden age of the British Empire, when we might encounter a scenario like this: "Yes, it's 7000 degrees in the shade. Yes, the natives are mounting an insurrection. Yes, I am running out of ammunition. And yes, there is a typhoon coming in, but dammit, man, I will have my tea and we will use the good china! What are we, animals?!?" We're joking, of course. But we understand that it can sometimes *feel* like blown-out diapers are less forgiving than typhoons, and one baby crying can be more panic-inducing than screaming warriors. We get it. And, of course it's okay to be flexible when you must. But rituals, especially those that you perform together, will anchor you and help you believe you will be okay.

Routines for Mom Care

Mom Rest Routines

Examples:

- Mom will nap when Baby naps.

- Dad will give Mom an hour for a nap when he comes home from work.

- Mom gets to sleep in while Dad takes Baby when getting ready for work in the mornings.

- On weekends, Dad gets up with Baby and Mom sleeps in.

- Dad handles nighttime diaper issues—especially if Mom is nursing!

Write your Mom rest routines here.

_____

_____

_____

Mom Nutrition Routines

Examples:

- On the weekends, Mom and Dad will put together several simple, healthy meals and store them in single-serving containers so that Mom can have nutritious lunches during the week.

- Dad will prepare a simple, healthy breakfast for Mom before he goes to work. She can eat it later, but it's ready for her each morning.

- You will buy healthier snacks rather than junk food when you go to the store in order to lessen the temptation to stress-eat.
- For those especially difficult days, you will keep a list of simple, quick, healthy dinners and the items needed to make them. If Mom's been home all day, you will agree that she's not allowed to feel guilty for asking Dad to do the cooking.

Write your Mom nutrition routines here.

_____

_____

_____

Mom Self-Care Routines

Examples:

- Dad will take "Baby duty" so Mom can shower each night.
- Dad will watch Baby while Mom showers before he leaves for work.
- If Dad can't be at home for Mom's shower, Mom will set the baby up in a baby seat outside the shower and play peek-a-boo from behind the shower curtain.
- Mom will have several easy-to-put-together, comfy outfits that she feels good about wearing.
- Mom will create a fast dress-and-makeup routine for days when she has little alone time.

Write your self-care routines here.

_____

_____

_____

CONNECTING RITUALS FOR NEW PARENTS

Work rituals help a new mom or dad avoid the feeling of having to handle all the chores alone. Even if it is something as simple as committing to putting the dishes away together every day, work rituals with your spouse can remind you that you have a partner who really is committed to helping you get through the day in one piece.

Play rituals, such as a game night, or a regular walk, or a date night (whether at home or out), remind you to make time—even just a few minutes—for a little fun. This way, on those days when you have pulled out your last hair and are calling your neighbors to see if you can start pulling out theirs, you might still find something to smile or even laugh about.

Talk rituals, such as a nightly commitment to touch base after Baby's asleep, or a daily commitment to chat while cleaning up the kitchen after dinner, can help you and your spouse remember that you are friends and why you've taken parenthood on in the first place.

Finally, *prayer rituals,* like a daily couple prayer time, remind you that God is in control even when you aren't. They help you let go of the stress, perfectionism, anxiety, and exhaustion most new parents feel and allow you to reconnect with the grace that will get you through another day.

The point isn't for routines and rituals to stress you out with one more thing you *have to* do to be a good parent. The point is that routines and rituals are good things to have in place so that you can create little oases of fun, connection, and harmony in what can otherwise be a very dry desert where self-care and marital intimacy (and we don't just mean sex) come last.

If you would like to get even more joy out of your growing family, take a moment to do the following exercise. Consider what simple rituals you and your spouse can create (or continue) so that you can connect through work, play, talk, and prayer. We offer some examples of rituals in each category and then ask you to identify at least one you will try to keep. Because things don't always go according to plan, especially with a new little one on the scene, we invite you to come up with a backup ritual for the days when your first choice just can't work out.

Working Together Rituals

Examples:

- Clean up the kitchen together after dinner while Baby is within sight, safe, and appropriately occupied.

- Fold laundry together while playing peek-a-boo with Baby.

- Straighten the family room together after Baby is asleep.

What will your working together rituals be?

You will need to be flexible. What is your fallback plan if Baby or something else prevents you from following through on this work ritual? For example, if your baby is too cranky to stay with you when you're folding laundry, perhaps one of you will finish the laundry while the other attends to Baby. Then, when Baby's calmer, you'll sort the bills together.

Playing Together Rituals

Examples:

- Play a favorite video game together when Baby is asleep.

- Play cards with each other while Baby takes a nursing break.

- Have one night a week where you make a special meal together and use the good dishes and candles—even as you're careful to keep the candles away from Baby.

What will your playing together rituals be?

What is your fallback plan? For example, if you can't get the preferred date night out, perhaps you can have a special dessert and watch a movie together at home.

Talking Together Rituals

Examples*:*

- Make time to talk together while giving Baby a bath.

- Make a lunchtime phone or Skype date during Baby's nap to check in with each other.

- Have breakfast together at least one weekday a week. (It's okay to go back to bed after breakfast if you're tired!)

What will your talking together rituals be?

What is your fallback plan? For example; if you can't connect on the phone over lunch, you'll make sure to call before leaving work so that you can catch each other up and discuss expectations about the rest of the evening.

Praying Together Rituals

Examples:

- Say the Rosary together (quietly) while Baby nurses or is rocked to sleep.

- Take time after dinner to pray together about the day and pray a blessing for Baby.

- Take a walk together with the baby in a stroller and pray while you walk.

What will your praying together rituals be?

What is your fallback plan? For example, if you can't take a prayer walk because it's raining, perhaps you can set the baby up with a snack or toy while you sit at the dinner table and pray.

Whatever you decide to do, these connecting rituals represent the bare-bones commitment you are making to take care of some of the most important aspects of your relationship together. Next, we look at some caregiver routines that can help make sure Mom gets her needs met too in the earliest weeks after giving birth.

What about Dad?

You might be wondering about dads. Why would we write these suggested routines and rituals under the assumption that Mom is *the* primary caregiver? First, because the baby has been bonding with Mom for nine months in the womb, listening to her voice and taking cues from her body on how to set his own biological rhythms, there is genuinely something unique and primary about Mom's care, especially in those first few weeks and months. Likewise, because family leave is more available to moms who work outside the home, it is more often they who provide the primary care of infants in the early weeks. As we explain later, dads must be as involved as possible from day one and will have needs of their own related to becoming a parent, but dads aren't interchangeable with moms, as many people think. Biologically, babies are wired to want Mom more—at least at first.

PART TWO

Enjoying Your New Arrival

Birth to Six Months

Babyhood is not what you think. Although this comes as a surprise to many parents, babyhood actually extends from birth to age three. That's because even though your child will go through remarkable leaps in development through the first three years, his or her brain is still primarily focused on the job of getting nerves and muscles to work together. The first three years of your child's life are all about working out the mind-to-body relationship. After age three, the emphasis is more and more on relating to the outside world with its expectations, rules, and obligations. Before age three, all of that is incidental.

Everything your little one goes through for the next three years—from newborn to late toddlerhood—will be about learning how to bring information into his brain and then getting his muscles (first the big ones such as arms and legs and then smaller ones such as fingers, mouth, and tongue) to respond to that information in intentional and conscious ways. As long as your child is focused on getting his body on line, he is considered to be a baby, neurologically speaking. Once a child has almost completely *mastered* the muscle control that makes walking, running, and talking in sentences possible (basically by the third year), then, and only then, does the stage of "early childhood" begin. At that point, he or she will start to learn how to get along with the outside world. Up until then, learning to get along with the outside world runs a distant second to learning to make brain and body work. This is important to know because too many parents wreck their joy of parenting by trying, too soon, to make interactions with their children all about following rules and enforcing someone else's standards.

Part two of *Then Comes Baby* consists of four chapters, each of which focuses on a different aspect of taking care of your child, yourself, or your marriage for the first six months of life with your baby.

Chapter 4 addresses baby care from birth to six months. What are the developmental milestones your baby should be achieving? What are the most joyful and loving ways you can handle feeding and sleeping, and what is the best way to get around—both in and out of the house—so that you can get the most out of both your parenting and the rest of your life?

Chapter 5 looks at mom care in the first six months after giving birth. We look at how Mom can make sure her needs are being met while still providing excellent care for your baby, and we help Dad and other family members know what kind of support they need to be giving the new mom.

Because parenting should bring husbands and wives closer to each other, chapter 6 offers some thoughts on caring for your marriage in those first months. We close part two with chapter 7, which explores how your child becomes part of God's family in Baptism. We offer some thoughts to consider in preparing for Baptism as well as some important insights about the spiritual care of your newborn that might surprise you.

CHAPTER FOUR

Getting to Know You!

When a woman is in labor, she is in anguish
because her hour has arrived;
but when she has given birth to a child,
she no longer remembers the pain
because of her joy that a child has been born
into the world.
—JOHN 16:21

You've just recently given birth and you're holding your little one in your arms. You are probably experiencing a rush of so many different emotions: joy, excitement, exhaustion, and not a little bit of anxiety. What an incredible gift you've been given! Of course, it means a lot of work too. In this chapter, we look at ways of responding to your baby's needs that make your life easier, more joyful, and more emotionally and spiritually satisfying to boot.

Lisa: I remember holding our first baby and being so surprised that I could love somebody so much so quickly. I know that for some moms, with exhaustion and the post-birth hormonal changes, it can take a little while for maternal feelings to kick in, but I was just struck by an overwhelming sense of love. I just wanted to give him the world.

Greg: One memory that stands out for me is holding our baby about a week after we came home from the hospital. I was trying to let Lisa have a nap (our first was a TERRIBLE sleeper). As I was holding him, I couldn't stop looking into his sweet, smiling face. He seemed so peaceful, so content. I don't think there is anything more precious than a baby's smile.

Your experience probably isn't much different from ours. You want to help your baby become everything God created her to be and you want to be everything your baby needs you to be. To get started, let's look at some of the questions you'll face about developmental milestones, feeding, sleep, and getting around with Baby. We also look at how bringing our Catholic faith to bear on your parenting decisions can help you create the kind of bond with your baby that enriches you emotionally, psychologically, and spiritually.

Developmental Milestones

> When I was a child, I used to talk as a child,
> think as a child, reason as a child.
> —1 Corinthians 13:11

Many parents treat developmental milestones as a test of how smart their baby is or find themselves secretly competing with other parents over whose child is superior. Normal parental pride notwithstanding, it is best to do whatever you can to resist these temptations since they just lead to a lot of unnecessary anxiety. The easiest way to take all the joy out of parenting is to make every day a test of how well you and your baby are measuring up. Instead of fretting, do your best to be grateful for the unique and unrepeatable child God has given you and rejoice in the little mysteries that unfold before your eyes each and every day!

Developmental milestones are loose guidelines that can give you a *general* sense of how well your baby is growing. There can be wide variations from baby to baby as far as when they achieve specific milestones. Regardless of the rate at which your baby is developing, the vast majority of children all catch up with each other eventually. By all means, you should discuss any persistent concerns with your pediatrician, but it's important to relax. Even if your child appears to be achieving some of the following milestones a little more slowly than some of your friends' children, babies grow and learn best in a calm and peaceful environment. We offer the following as a guide to help you know more or less what to expect in the first six months. Just remember, your most important job is to enjoy getting to know your little treasure through and through. That means spending lots and lots of time together with your baby, being extravagantly affectionate, and laughing with and enjoying your baby as much as possible. Have fun with your little one and, for the most part, everything else will eventually fall into place.

Motor Milestones

The vast majority of the human brain develops after birth, and basic motor control is the first thing babies work overtime to learn. A newborn's first physical task is learning to get his nerves and muscles to work together. Remember, this will be your baby's primary occupation, in various forms, for the first three years of life.

In the first few weeks after birth, your baby's head will be a little wobbly, but by three months, most babies develop enough nerve and muscle tone and coordination to lift up their heads when lying on their backs. Also in the first three months, babies are working toward being able to roll from back to side (though not all the way over from back to front). While babies' nerves and muscles are first learning to work together, their movements are jerky and sporadic. From birth to three months, your baby will be figuring out how to get his nerves to tell his muscles to make his motions more intentional. By three months old, many babies are able to more purposefully grasp a toy that you hold out and hang on to it for several moments.

From four to six months your baby's quest to connect his nerves and muscles will continue through the process of pushing up on all fours as a prelude to crawling. When your child is ready to begin this process, you'll start noting better head control and your baby will start working to roll over onto his or her tummy. Pretty soon, your little one is going to be crawling up a storm!

Sensory Milestones (Hearing and Vision)

In the first weeks after birth, your newborn's hearing is still developing, but even brand-new babies will startle if they hear a loud noise. Likewise, your baby will probably show signs of recognizing your voices since she been listening to them and bonding to them for nine months in Mom's womb. The familiar sound of Mom's voice in particular is very comforting to the newborn, who has so many new sights and sounds to get used to. After spending nine months in a warm, dark, and cuddly place, there are so many new things to take in! Talking softly and soothingly to your baby and letting your baby warm up to new environments (and people) slowly are some of the best things you can do to comfort and encourage her as she learns about this bright new world she has been born into.

Newborns tend to be able to see only the distance from Mom's breast to her face (about five to eighteen inches). Babies are fascinated by faces, especially the face that is attached to the voice she's been listening to in the womb and (if you are nursing) that accompanies the comfort of feeding. Newborns are also very curious about their hands and feet. You'll probably see your little scholar studying hers a lot. By three months, most babies are interested in more complex patterns and will focus their eyes on specific things that grab their attention.

From four to six months, your baby's vision becomes clearer. She will start to distinguish between strange and familiar faces and be attracted to bright colors. If you roll a ball across the floor, she will be more and more likely to follow it with her eyes.

Communication Milestones

Even though babies aren't big talkers, communication is very important to them. You could probably call the first language babies learn *face talk*. Face talk is the rudimentary, nonverbal language of facial expressions, gestures, and emotions. The more you look at your baby and keep him close to your face—by nursing or "wearing" your newborn in a sling, for instance—the more opportunities you give your baby to study your face and try to get his facial nerves and muscles to work together and match your expressions. Watching and matching facial expressions is a game most babies never get tired of. It takes a lot of study to get this right, but by two months, many babies will know how to smile on purpose and will have discovered subtler ways (subtler, that is, than wailing) of getting your attention. Common discoveries at this stage are learning how to coo and reach for a caretaker when he wants your care or needs soothing.

From four to six months, your baby is developing a whole language of babbling and cooing sounds. These sounds are the building blocks of what will eventually become actual words. Your little one might also start playing little language games with you, like babbling and then waiting for you to say something before he starts babbling again.

Developmental Milestones: What Can You Do?

While it seems magical to watch newborns achieve their milestones, there's a lot of physiological development occurring.

It's hard work for newborns to teach their nerves and muscles to work together, and they truly appreciate any help parents can give them. There are many things you can do.

In his teachings of the theology of the body, John Paul II showed us how we can learn a great deal about God's intention for how we relate as men and women by prayerfully attending to the design of our bodies.[1] The more you learn about the way God designed your baby's brain and body to grow, the more you will be able to respond to your child in a manner that helps this process along. When it comes to parenting babies, the best way to take all the joy out of your life is to try to force your little one to comply with external, cookie-cutter rules, schedules, and expectations he or she isn't neurologically ready to accommodate. When you stop trying to force your baby to fit into grown-up boxes and instead align your expectations with God's design of your baby's brain and body, you will all be less stressed out and enjoy your baby's infancy more.

Learning to change and grow in response to your baby's cues can become in your spiritual life what St. Thérèse of Lisieux called the "little way" of holiness. This little way consists of doing small things with great love, especially if those small things require a bit of sacrifice on our part. Attending generously to your child's signs and needs can be hard work, but the payoff is great in terms of the peace and connection parents and infants can enjoy. The spiritual benefits you will receive as parents will make the effort deeply gratifying.

Let's look at how you can respond to your baby in ways that make your life easier and more pleasant and help your baby thrive contentedly.

Extravagant Affection

We're going to let you in on a secret. You cannot hold, cuddle, or caress your baby too much. In fact, it's hard to hold babies enough! God made babies to stay close to Mom and Dad. Brain science shows that affection—and "extravagant" affection in particular—helps babies' brains grow more.[2] What do we mean by *extravagant*? Well, if someone tells you that you're spoiling your baby by holding him "too much," you've probably got it just about right. According to research, only 6 percent of babies are receiving the amount of affection they need to let their social brain (those combined brain structures that help us participate in and enjoy the benefits of our connection with others) grow to its full potential.[3] The same study, which followed participants from infancy to their mid-thirties, found that the 85 percent of infants and toddlers who received "normal" levels of affection were significantly more likely to be anxious and unsatisfied in their life and relationships as adults than those participants who had received "extravagant" levels of affection in infancy and toddlerhood.

Newborn babies function best when they have almost constant contact with their moms. This helps them adjust to the very confusing fact that they used to be inside you and now they are outside you. That's kind of a shocking reality. Keeping Baby close makes her feel much more at peace with the dramatic change in scenery and allows her nervous system and senses to come on line more efficiently.

> **Lisa:** For me, there is nothing like holding my little one in my arms, seeing her smiles, kissing her face, putting my face up to her head and smelling her. From the work and research Greg and I do, I know that holding your baby close releases hormones in your body that lift your mood and help you feel close your child. But on a personal level, all I can tell you is that it feels great. There are few joys that compare to having close cuddle time with my babies. It's wonderful to think that as much as I enjoy it, they enjoy it even more!

Remember—and we can't say this enough because it's hard for parents to remember—babies don't actually realize that you aren't just part of them. That's especially true for newborns, who have lived a whole lot longer inside and as part of your body than they have outside of and separate from you. As the renowned pediatrician Dr. Bill Sears has said, it's a good idea to think of pregnancy as nine months in the womb and nine months out.[4] Your baby will eventually learn to be his own person, but first he has to get used to his world being turned inside out—literally. Generously holding and cuddling your baby lets him get comfortably used to being in the outside world.

Physical contact is essential for brain growth. Holding your baby stimulates his senses and releases relaxing hormones that promote more efficient neural connectivity and learning. Always remember: a calm, cuddled baby is a happy, *learning* baby.[5] The more you cuddle and carry your child, the more you are teaching him everything he needs to know about feeling right within himself while he is mastering those first lessons of intentional movement and the language of "face talk."

All this holding is going to make your life infinitely easier and more peaceful because a cuddled baby is a happy baby, and happy, unstressed babies don't cry nearly as much as babies who are put down. Trust us, the less your baby cries, the happier and less stressed your parenting life will be.[6] So make it easy on yourself. Follow your heart. Hold your baby as much as you want and enjoy the experience of being close to the incredible gift God gave you.

Baby Talk

Be sure to talk to your baby. Newborns love to listen to and learn from the sound of your voice. Your voice is both comforting and educational. Talk softly and gently. Use baby talk and, as much as possible, look at your baby when speaking. Babies love and need lots and lots of eye contact. Make big, somewhat exaggerated faces. They are easier to learn to mimic. Much of this comes naturally to many parents. If it does for you, go with it. If not, a little practice goes a long way!

Respond Promptly to Cries

Remember, a calm, cuddled baby is a happy, *learning* baby. Babies who are stressed and crying are not learning; the brain locks down and neural development is put on pause until comfort is reacquired.[7] By responding promptly to your baby's cries, you help your child spend his energy on his developmental task of learning, growing, and developing instead of crying hard to get your attention. Both can be hard work, but only the first should be necessary.

Besides, let's face it—infant crying is tough to listen to. It's supposed to be. It means something is wrong and requires our attention. Ignoring infant crying feels unnatural because it is. Responding promptly to Baby's cries is good not just for Baby's nerves, but for grown-up nerves too!

Greg: As a musician, I'm very sensitive to sound and noise, and to be completely honest, a baby's crying is like nails on a chalkboard to me. In the apartment we lived in when we had our first two children, the bathroom was so tiny you could sit on the toilet and rest your head on the opposite wall. Sometimes, no matter how attentive you are, while a baby's senses are still coming on line and he or she is struggling to learn those first ways of communicating with you through expressions, sounds, and gestures, the child can be inconsolable. One time, during an extended crying jag one of our little ones was having, I had to ask Lisa to excuse me for a minute to use the restroom and calm my rattled nerves. I sat down on the toilet, covered my ears and bounced my head against the wall a few times in exasperation. Obviously, I had a strong motivation for helping our children learn that they didn't have to cry to get our attention.

When I first started my private practice, I was seeing clients in our home. A few months after this incident that had me retreating to the bathroom, a client commented to me that she never heard our baby cry. She jokingly wondered if Lisa was hiding in an upstairs closet or something. I explained that our son did cry, that in fact he tended to cry a lot when he was a newborn (although I didn't tell her the bathroom story). I explained that by keeping him close and paying attention to subtler cues like facial expressions and sounds, we were slowly trying to teach him that he didn't have to cry, at least not loudly or long, to get our attention or to have his needs met. I explained that, happily, it seemed to be working for all of us—baby, parents, and clients. My client actually began to tear up at that. She said that my explanation touched something deep inside her and made her realize that real love—the kind she ached for—truly did exist. She said that something about my response helped her connect in that moment with how God must love her. I was a little stunned. I like to say that God wants to change the world through our families, and this is one of the moments that taught me how true it is. I'll never forget how simply relating the way Lisa and I responded to our babies created a real healing and transformational moment for that woman.

We want to be clear. We are *not* saying that horrible things will happen if your baby ever cries. Not at all! Babies cry. We do what we can, but it happens. What we are saying is that medical research consistently shows that prompt parental response to infant crying facilitates good parent-baby relationships and helps babies grow best.[8] Sometimes crying can't be helped—at least for a little while—and that's okay. You will all survive (we promise). Just don't make the mistake of thinking that crying is somehow normal or desirable. It is neither. Likewise, don't listen to people who tell you that you will spoil your baby by responding too much to his cries. Imagine if you were completely incapable of meeting even the simplest need you had. How would it feel to have someone ignore you when you tried to ask for help? How would it feel to call and have no one come? What would that feel like? That's how it feels to your baby if you don't respond to his cries.

One conventional, but thankfully fading, way of getting a baby to stop crying is to ignore him until he learns that there is no point in crying any more. That's certainly one way to do it, but there is a gentler way. What if, by keeping your baby close and responding as quickly as reasonably possible to her fussing, you could help your child learn a vocabulary of facial expressions, sounds, and gestures that would enable her to communicate with you *without* crying? Not only would your child cry less, but you two would have grown closer. That's the kind of win-win that applying the principle of the common good to parenting can help you achieve.

PLAYING WITH YOUR INFANT

> Waste time with your children!
> —Pope Francis

From birth to six months, your child's best toy is you! Your child is learning through touch, sound, and close-up sight. He or she is craving close contact with you. Face-to-face close contact with you as you coo, smile, and laugh will light up your child's life.

- *Singing* is a wonderful way to interact with your baby. Sing and dance with your child in your arms. It's a great way to lift your spirits and entertain your baby.

- *Rattles* and toys with chimes are great ways to engage your child's attention and help your little one practice tracking (i.e., intentional eye movement).

- *Soft toys* that crinkle or squeak can engage your baby's attention and help you interact.

- *Infant massage* is a wonderful way to relax your little one, stimulate his or her muscles, and help you maintain skin-to-skin contact.

- Good *old-fashioned games* like peek-a-boo or itsy bitsy spider are classics because they engage your little one through sight and sound.

- Carrying your little one in a *sling* allows you to maintain visual and auditory contact while easily providing the rocking motion infants crave.

Feeding

> He was lofty but he sucked Mary's milk, and from his blessings all creation sucks. He is the Living Breast of living breath; by His life the dead were suckled, and they revived. . . . As indeed He sucked Mary's milk, He has given suck—life—to the universe.
>
> —St. Ephrem the Syrian

Most of you are probably aware of the benefits breast-feeding gives your baby, and we talk about those in a moment, but breast-feeding can also make your life as a parent easier and more enjoyable.

Breast-Feeding Benefits Mom

On average nursing moms get more sleep, are healthier, and have brighter moods than bottle-feeding moms.[9] When you breast-feed, every single time you nurse, your body releases hormones that decrease your stress level and make you feel closer and more in love with your baby.[10] Even more interesting, new research that looks at the brain function of breast-feeding moms shows that nursing actually strengthens the parts of the maternal brain that make you both *feel* like a more competent mom and *actually* be a more competent mom by fine-tuning your nervous system to respond more quickly and make better sense of your baby's cues.[11] In his theology of the body, John Paul II referred to this ability of the woman's body to adapt in a way that not only creates life but also responds to and nurtures it so perfectly as "the feminine genius."[12] The more you cooperate with God's design of your body, the more you turn on all the resources God has given you to help you be the mom he wants you to be, the mom your baby needs you to be, the mom your heart is calling you to be. And that feels great!

> **Lisa:** I can remember lots of times when I felt wrung out as a new mom. Often it had nothing to do with the baby. Sometimes it was the house getting to me. Other times it was missing my family. Still other times it was messages I was sending myself, like "I don't know what I'm doing. What if I'm getting everything all wrong?" It doesn't really matter. On those days, I was so grateful to be able to nurse my babies. Every time I sat down to nurse, all the noise would stop. My mind would quiet down, the baby would settle down, and somehow everything seemed more manageable. I don't mean to overstate it: nursing isn't magic, of course. But it was such a help to me. Nursing—especially nursing on request—helped me feel so much more connected to our babies. And it forced me to sit down and take care of myself. Without nursing, it would have been so easy for me to push myself to the breaking point trying to get

everything done. When I nursed, I could just close my eyes and breathe. It required me to look into my baby's eyes and remember that everything was going to be okay. Those were wonderful, intimate, peaceful moments that helped me connect to my motherhood on such a deeply personal level. I know my babies got a lot out of it, but it did wonderful things for me as well. For me, nursing wasn't about being my baby's vending machine. It was about sharing a loving embrace with my baby that nourished us both—body and soul—and reminded me that nothing is more important—not chores, not errands, not anything—than that loving connection God calls us to enjoy with him and share with one another. There is nothing more restorative than that.

Beyond the physiological and psychological benefits moms get from nursing, it's just easier on a practical level.

Lisa: The other reason I loved nursing was that it enabled me to be so much more "portable" than I might otherwise have been. Having to pack bottles and formula and haul all that stuff around was exhausting when I did so for our adopted daughter. It made me think twice about leaving the house in ways I never did when I was able to nurse our other children. With the babies I nursed, I could just pop them in the baby sling and head out the door with a few diapers in my purse. I didn't need a small army of attendants and a quartermaster to manage all my gear. It was simply the baby and me. With a little practice, a good nursing bra, and my baby sling, I could nurse discreetly almost anywhere. On those days I needed to get out, it was terrific to know I could just head out the door without having to make a list and check it twice. Having done both, I can say hands down that nursing is a thousand times easier than bottle-feeding, and the longer you do it, the easier it gets.

Breast-Feeding Benefits Baby

When it comes to your baby, there is simply no question that by every measure—physiological, emotional, psychological, relational, and even (believe it or not) spiritual—breast *is* best. The American Academy of Pediatrics recommends exclusive breast-feeding for six months and recommends continuing breast-feeding for twelve months or longer if mom and baby are willing and able. Even toddlers receive many physiological and psychological benefits from nursing. Here are some things you might be surprised to learn about breast milk and the nursing relationship.

Breast milk is easier to digest than formula and is specifically created to facilitate human brain growth. Even more importantly, breast milk is *living food*. It actually changes according to the nurser's needs.[13] For instance, if you or your baby is sick, breast milk will carry antibodies between you and your baby to fight infection. If a mom is nursing two children (e.g., a toddler and an infant), the milk will actually be different depending on which child is nursing.[14] Nursing teaches your baby his first important lessons about self-monitoring food intake. In fact, nursing allows every baby to have ongoing communication with Mom about what the baby wants to eat, how much, and when. In his book *My Child Won't Eat*, pediatrician Dr. Carlos González writes that when you nurse,

> Your child has at his disposal a large selection of "menu" items from which to choose, from a light soup to a creamy dessert. Since the breast can't talk, the baby puts in his order three ways: (1) by the amount of milk he drinks at each feeding (that is, nursing for a shorter or longer amount of time, and with more or less

intensity), (2) by the interval between one feeding and the next, and (3) by drinking from one
or both breasts.

What your child does at the breast to obtain
exactly what he needs from one day to the next
is pure engineering. The child has total and
perfect control over his diet as long as he can
change the variables at will. . . . When a child is
not allowed to control one of the mechanisms,
most of the time he manages an adequate diet
by maneuvering the other two variables.[15]

Breast-Feeding Basics

Even the best-quality formula cannot compete with the
dynamic nature of breast milk and the nursing relationship.
There are too many benefits to be gained from nursing for
both mother and baby to go into detail here. We list several
resources in chapter 18 that will answer additional questions
and help you overcome any challenges you might face in the
nursing relationship. But we do want to address a few things
you need to know up front in order to successfully breast-feed.

Proper latch-on. For many women who feel they cannot
nurse or experience painful nursing, the problem is often
caused by the baby's incorrect latch-on. If the baby is just suck-
ing on your nipple, nursing is both inefficient and painful. You
will need to make sure that your baby's mouth completely surrounds your areola (the darker circle around your nipple). To
latch your baby on properly, gently squeeze your breast about
an inch or two behind your areola. Then, tickle the baby's lips
with your nipple. When your baby opens her mouth, *quickly
and confidently insert both your nipple and areola* into the baby's
mouth. The baby should take care of the rest from there.

Nursing pain is never normal. It is always a sign that there
is a problem that needs to be corrected. The good news is that

there are very few nursing problems that do not respond to treatment. The key is getting the right kind of support. It is very important that you work with a trained and certified lactation consultant if you are having difficulties. *Lactation consultants*—even more than your pediatrician, who may not have received any training at all in the anatomy of the breast or proper nursing practices—are the professionals who are best equipped to help you establish and maintain a healthy nursing relationship with your baby.[16] With proper training and support, the overwhelming majority of women are able to nurse well and painlessly.

Feeding frequency. Trust your child, not a schedule. Letting your child dictate the frequency and duration of feeding is best for the long-term diet, nutrition, and general health of your child. Assuming your child is gaining weight and regularly urinating and having bowel movements, all is well. Do not put your nursing baby on a schedule unless your circumstances absolutely require it and you are directed to do so by a lactation consultant or nursing-friendly pediatrician.[17] If you are nursing, you should *especially* not use feeding schedules produced for formula-fed babies. Formula is harder to digest and therefore takes longer to digest than breast milk, so formula-fed babies eat less frequently. Putting nursing babies on any schedule, especially a formula-based schedule, can cause nutritional concerns for Baby and/or early drying up of your milk.

Many moms think they need to put their babies on a schedule because of their fear of nursing in public. The thought of nursing in front of others can be intimidating for new moms, but as Pope Francis recently pointed out, moms and dads need only worry about their baby's needs, not the inappropriate squeamishness of those around them. Can you imagine anything more intimidating than nursing in front of the pope? And yet Pope Francis related this story about his encouragement to a nervous, nursing mom:

> There are so many children that cry because they
> are hungry. At the Wednesday General Audience
> the other day there was a young mother behind
> one of the barriers with a baby that was just a
> few months old. The child was crying its eyes
> out as I came past. The mother was caressing it. I
> said to her: "Madam, I think the child's hungry."
> "Yes, it's probably time . . . ," she replied. "Please
> give it something to eat!" I said. She was shy
> and didn't want to breast-feed in public, while
> the Pope was passing. I wish to say the same to
> humanity: give people something to eat! That
> woman had milk to give to her child; we have
> enough food in the world to feed everyone.[18]

Trust your baby to tell you when he is hungry and how hungry he is—even if you're visiting with the pope (or your mother-in-law)! Arbitrary, cookie-cutter feeding schedules make your baby cranky and your life more stressful as you put yourself in a position in which you are constantly at war with your God-given instincts. Assuming your baby is normal and healthy, God built into your child a completely self-regulating system with regard to feeding, and he created Mom's body to respond powerfully to Baby's desire to nurse when she asks for it. Just as you cannot spoil your baby by holding her "too much," you can't cause problems by nursing as often as your baby asks. In fact, the opposite is true. Infant-directed nursing is safe and natural, and it is part of the dialogue between mother and baby that promotes good bonding and attachment as well as healthy future eating habits.[19] When you make yourself available to nurse based on your infant's request, you facilitate a loving, trusting relationship that helps the baby have confidence in your ability to consistently and generously meet her needs.[20] This has extraordinarily positive ramifications for your child's physiological, emotional, psychological, relational, and spiritual because a healthy faith life is founded on a deep and abiding *physical* sense of trust.[21]

In his theology of the body, John Paul II reminds us that if we prayerfully reflect upon God's design of our body we can learn a great deal of God's intention for our relations with others.[22] Why does God give mothers breast milk? Whom is it for? The mother? Clearly not. Breast milk is God's gift to the child. The mother simply holds this gift in trust for the child. God gives Mom this perfect food so that the child can be nourished physically, psychologically, relationally, and spiritually. And when Mom gives her baby what is rightfully his, she receives the wash of hormones that give her a sense of peace, connectedness, and confidence that comes from cooperating with God's parenting plan. When you trust your body, you allow God to work through your body to facilitate all the benefits God wishes to give you and your child.

If I Can't Nurse, Am I a Failure?

The short answer is "No, of course not." No matter how much you may be tempted to feel otherwise, feeding your baby is not a test and you cannot pass or fail it. Nursing can be a terrific help to Mom's peace of mind, but you can still feel great about your motherhood even if you can't nurse. Nursing does make mothering easier, but not nursing doesn't make great mothering impossible. Parents need to remember that feeding is about meeting your baby's needs and not about validating your egos. Don't make this about you. In fact, the more you make this about proving your competence as a mom, the harder it may be to establish a healthy nursing relationship.

That said, because nursing is so beneficial to both Baby and Mom, it is important to seek early help to overcome any challenges you or Baby might be experiencing in the nursing relationship. A certified lactation consultant should be your first person to consult with any nursing problems. The resources in chapter 18 will help you find competent help. If however, you face either physical or relational problems (e.g., poor support, inflexible work environment) that cannot be overcome through reasonable means and persistently undermine the nursing relationship, bottle-feeding is perfectly adequate for infant nutrition and can be done in a way that promotes healthy bonding.

> **Lisa:** When we adopted our third child, from China, she was fourteen months old but as small as a six-month-old because of malnutrition. Before we brought her home, a part of me really wanted to try to nurse with a supplemental nursing system (SNS) because I knew that up to 50 percent of adoptive mothers can stimulate the let-down reflex and nurse their adopted babies to some extent with an SNS. I loved nursing our other children and valued how much it had helped our bond and made my life easier, but given our daughter's age, it wasn't practically possible to try. She needed me to be present to her, and feeding her had to be about responding to her needs, not fulfilling my desires. So, instead, we used the best-quality formula that was commonly available, and I created bottle-feeding rituals to help make bottle-feeding as close to nursing as possible. Although my bottle-feeding experience was with a slightly older, adopted child, everything I did is easily transferable and equally important for getting the most out of bottle-feeding a newborn.
>
> Because feeding is such an important part of attachment (a baby's learning who the primary person is to whom she can turn for meeting her needs), I made sure that I was the only one feeding her for at least the first several months. I let her tell me when and how long she wanted to eat. All babies are very good at this. A person has to actually be taught to

eat poorly by learning to ignore internal hunger cues in order to conform to external schedules.

When she indicated that she was hungry or even if she just needed a bottle for security, I had her sit on my lap and lie in the crook of my arm just like I was going to nurse her. I would hold the bottle at breast level, and while she ate, I looked into her eyes and talked soothingly, or sang to her, just as if she were nursing. It was a beautiful experience for both of us. She was mine, and I was hers, and nothing could change that. She was learning that any time she needed comfort or food, I was the person she could consistently trust to generously meet that need.

Was it exactly the same as nursing? Well, no. In some ways, it was much more difficult than nursing. Carting around bottles and formula wherever I went was a real pain, and there were other important differences I was sensitive to since I nursed my other babies. But that wasn't the important thing. The important thing was that I was doing everything my circumstances allowed me to do to bond with my baby and give her what she needed to develop that deep, physical sense that I would always be the one she could turn to meet her needs whenever and whatever they were. This is what she needed to grow up to become the loving, secure, attached person God created her to be.

Spirituality and Infant Feeding

> Like newborn infants, long for pure spiritual
> milk so that through it you may grow into
> salvation, for you have tasted that the Lord
> is good.
>
> —1 PETER 2:2–3

Whether you breast-feed or bottle-feed, it is critical to remember that, as far as your baby is concerned, feeding is not just about food. More importantly, feeding is about giving your baby every opportunity to learn that he can trust you to meet his needs generously and consistently; looking into each other's eyes and learning to read each other's cues; and helping your baby discover that you (primarily) have that special touch that can make him feel safe, peaceful, and at home in your arms when his world seems out of synch or overwhelming.

You might be surprised to learn that prior to the Reformation, the predominant Christian image of God's compassion for humanity was not the crucifixion, but the nursing Madonna.[23] Devotion to "Maria Lactans" (the Nursing Mother) was extremely common among early Christians. So-called "milk shrines" sprang up across the Christian world as a sign of reverence to the Blessed Mother, who was known as the "wet nurse of salvation" (because she nursed Jesus, who is our salvation). One of the most famous stories from the life of St. Bernard of Clairvaux, illustrated by many artists over the centuries, has the Blessed Mother squirting milk into St. Bernard's mouth from her breast as a sign of both her motherhood of all humanity and her commitment to give him the milk of divine wisdom.

The early Church Fathers often made beautiful comparisons between a nursing mother and the Blessed Sacrament. Though such comparisons may sound foreign to our ears, they are certainly appropriate. God feeds his children with his own body and uses the Eucharist, that most intimate of meals, to intimately bond us to him. In light of this wisdom, it would not be unreasonable to say that infant feeding in general can be a first catechesis that teaches the most important foundational faith lesson: When I reach out, someone will always be there to satisfy both my deepest hunger and my longing for connection with one who is beyond me.

Infant Sleep

This is one area where parents make things much more difficult for themselves than is necessary. Getting your baby to sleep should not be a source of stress and frustration. Babies sleep when they need to sleep. The more you try to force your own ideas of how your baby "ought" to sleep and the ways things "should" be because of some cookie-cutter schedule someone told you your baby should be following, the more oppressed you will feel and the more your baby will fight you. Stop the insanity! Trust God's design of your baby. Remember the theology of the body. Your baby was not designed to be away from you. The farther away from you your baby stays at night, the more difficulty you will have getting your baby to sleep and keeping your baby asleep once he finally decides to visit Dreamland.

Nighttime Parenting Considerations

Parents have many available options when it comes to deciding the best way to manage infant sleep. As you consider your choices, especially if you are trying to parent with God's design of your baby in mind, let's recall what we know so far.

1. Extravagant affection is healthy and facilitates the development of the social brain.

2. Prompt response to infant crying teaches the baby basic trust and helps the baby learn to regulate the calm-down mechanisms of his or her nervous system.

3. Crying is not normal or healthy. It is always a sign that something in the baby's world is out of balance and that the child needs Mom and/or Dad's help getting things back in balance.

4. Formulating basic trust is the first spiritual lesson parents teach babies. Responding promptly to infant cries teaches children on a gut level (literally) that when they call out, someone will respond. This is a terrifically important lesson for Catholic parents who want their children to have confidence that God is present and responsive in their lives. ("On the day I cried out, you answered; you strengthened my spirit" [Psalm 138:3]).

Additionally, the idea that babies should sleep eight to ten hours per night is a myth. There is simply no healthy way to get a baby to sleep this long at a stretch. You can force your baby to sleep at longer stretches, but forcing is exactly what you would be doing. The process for accomplishing this unnatural feat is both emotionally and physically exhausting for parents and completely contrary to your baby's nature. The newborn's brain has not developed to the point of having circadian rhythms (regular day and night cycles). Newborns tend to sleep up to sixteen hours a day in two- to four-hour stretches. Consequently, there is no question that it is possible to get the rest *you* need if you are intentional about it. You may well be able to coax a little more sleep time out of your baby by nursing her to sleep (a full tummy aids sleep) or by keeping your baby near you at night, which helps stabilize her bodily systems and enables you to quiet her quickly without her having to wake as much. But *managing your expectations* is the most important part of dealing with the challenge of infant sleep schedules. By six months, the average baby will sleep for longer stretches (about six hours at a time), but still may not sleep completely through the night. Up through the first year, and even after, many children wake at least once or twice per night. This is perfectly normal, and the sooner you make your peace with it, the happier you will be.

The most important thing you can do to handle any disruptions in your regular sleep patterns is to nap when Baby naps. Don't use that time for chores. The most important chores a new mom has are (1) taking care of Baby and (2) taking care of herself.

> **Lisa:** As we've mentioned, our first child was a terrible sleeper. I remember sitting up for what seemed like hours watching the shopping channel at three in the morning because nothing else was on. The only thing that saved me was getting naps when he slept during the day. And Greg was a huge help. He didn't make me feel guilty for not having the house in perfect order or not having dinner cooked when he got home. He'd call throughout the day so that we could stay in touch and he would know what to expect when he got home. I was so grateful that he jumped right in to clean, cook, or do whatever else needed to be done. I sometimes felt horribly guilty about this.

> **Greg:** I know Lisa felt guilty about my pitching in with the house, but I honestly never understood it. Bonding with a baby is wonderful, but it can also be hard and exhausting work. It is the most important thing she could ever do. Bonding well with Baby prevents so many difficulties later on. Doing the kind of work I do, I see the effects of poor parent-child bonding all the time. I really appreciated that the work Lisa was putting into taking care of our babies was saving us loads of trouble later on!

> **Lisa:** Even so, it meant the world to me. His giving me the help I needed kept me sane, especially the first time around. Somehow it was easier with our

other kids. I guess a lot of that had to do with experience and having a better idea of what to expect and
how to manage it. But knowing that I could always
count on Greg to do whatever I needed him to do to
get me the rest and the care I needed to stay sane
made it possible for me to focus on being there for
our babies no matter what they needed.

Beyond napping when Baby naps and farming out household chores to your spouse or outside help, here are some
additional recommendations for infant sleeping arrangements.

Keep Baby as Close as Possible

Keeping the baby in your room is the most efficient sleep
solution for babies and parents. When a baby sleeps in your
room, you hear his cries sooner so you can attend to them more
quickly. That means that neither you nor the baby has to wake
up as much as you would have to if the baby were in another
room having to cry more loudly to get your attention and you
were having to walk all the way to the other room to attend
to him. Ironically, waking earlier to Baby's fussing gets both
parents and Baby back to sleep faster.

Co-Sleeping/Bed Sharing

Some parents choose to sleep with their baby in their bed. This
is known as *co-sleeping* or *bed sharing*. We highly recommend
this practice. Most parents will have babies or children in their
bed at one point or another, and researchers like Dr. James
McKenna argue that it is not only harmless, but quite beneficial.[24] Since co-sleeping is so beneficial, we believe that it is
better to be intentional about it than to have erratic sleep rituals
that confuse both Baby and parents.

When you co-sleep, if the baby needs to nurse or be
comforted at night, it is a simple matter to roll over, nurse
or otherwise comfort the child, and go back to sleep. In this

arrangement, the baby rarely wakes fully and so is much easier to quiet. Bed sharing allows you to maximize physical contact with your child, respond most promptly to your child's cries, help your child quickly restore any imbalances he or she may be experiencing, and get back to sleep more quickly than any other arrangement.

> **Lisa:** It was such a blessing to co-sleep with our babies. They never had to wake up to the point of crying to get my attention. Even our worst sleeper—once I finally got him down in the first place—cuddled right up and went back to sleep if I responded quickly enough and nursed him. It was the same with the daughter we bottle-fed. Having our children close allowed me to quickly give them the comfort and nourishment they needed to get back to sleep and also let me get the rest I needed.

Some parents worry that the baby will suffocate with co-sleeping. Because of this concern, some pediatricians recommend against the practice, but there is in no way universal agreement among experts on this issue. Co-sleeping experts, like pediatrician and author Dr. Bill Sears and Dr. James McKenna of the University of Notre Dame Mother-Infant Sleep Lab, agree that co-sleeping is safe as long as common safe bed sharing practices are employed.[25] Despite media claims to the contrary, there is no medical evidence to suggest that parents who follow recommended safe co-sleeping practices are placing their babies at risk.[26] In fact, a recent professional review of all the literature for and against co-sleeping called condemnations of the practice both unethical and unhelpful.[27] Of course, all parenting practices should be conducted safely. Here are some common recommendations for safe bed sharing:

1. Place the baby on his back, never on his tummy or side. (This is also true if you opt for crib sleeping.)

2. Do not place the child on a pillow or on any other fluffy sleeping surface that could cause suffocation. Do not place soft stuffed animals around the child, as this is also a suffocation hazard. All of these cautions also apply to crib sleeping.

3. Under normal circumstances, parents do not roll over on their babies. However, DO NOT sleep on the same surface as your baby if you are obese, if you are on sedatives, if you smoke, or if you have been drinking. All of these circumstances could result in *overlay*, in which a parent unknowingly rolls over on a child. If any of these circumstances apply to you, you should not attempt bed sharing with your baby. Instead, we recommend either using a co-sleeper that butts up against your bed for the easiest approach to nighttime parenting or having the crib in your room.

4. Co-sleep ONLY in a bed, NEVER on a sofa or other piece of furniture where the baby could become wedged between you and the furniture.

Crib Sleeping

Crib sleeping also carries risks. A study by Nationwide Children's Hospital Center for Injury Research and Policy found that crib-related injuries are responsible for 10,000 emergency room visits and 100 infant deaths per year in the United States.[28] This same study recommends the following practices for safe crib sleeping:

1. Select a crib that meets all current safety standards, does not have a drop side, and is not old or broken.

2. Avoid cribs with cutouts, decorative corner posts, or knobs that stick up more than 1/16 inch.

3. Use caution when considering a secondhand crib. It may have been recalled or be missing parts or instructions.

4. Check for crib recalls at www.recalls.gov.

5. If you can fit more than two fingers between the mattress and the crib frame, you need a bigger mattress.

6. The slats of the crib should be no more than two and three-eighths inches apart. A baby's head could get trapped in more widely spaced slats.

7. When putting the crib together, carefully read and follow all assembly instructions.

8. Cover the mattress with a snug-fitting crib sheet.

9. Check the crib often for loose or missing pieces.

10. Remove any hanging toys or mobiles when the baby is able to get up on all fours.

11. When your child can pull herself up or stand, adjust the mattress to its lowest position. The crib sides should be at least twenty-six inches above the mattress support to prevent falls.

12. Check the manufacturer's instructions to know when your child will outgrow the crib.

13. Place cribs and other nursery furniture away from windows, and keep cords from window blinds, shades, and baby monitors out of reach. If possible, use cordless window coverings.

14. Bare cribs are best. Do not put pillows, blankets, sleep positioners, bumper pads or stuffed toys in the crib with the baby. Use sleepers or sleep sacks instead of blankets to keep the baby warm.

15. Never put a baby to sleep on a soft surface such as a waterbed, sofa, soft mattress, or pillow. Babies should sleep on their backs on a firm mattress.

16. Crib tents and canopies are not safe to use over cribs.

Additional Sleeping Options

If you would prefer not to bring Baby to bed, but have your concerns about cribs, then we would suggest a co-sleeper that rests next to your bed, or at least keeping your baby in the room with you. The point is that the farther away your child is from you, the harder your baby has to work to get your attention, the more awake everyone is, and the harder it is to get both you and Baby back to sleep. Remember that the Bible tells us that "it is not good for . . . man to be alone" (Gen 2:18). We were created to be in contact with others. A newborn baby is not neurologically equipped to be alone at any time, day or night. Although it is romantic to think of your baby sleeping soundly in a perfectly decorated nursery, this is simply not the best arrangement for Baby. A nursery is a great play space, but it is not ideal, either for Baby or for parents, for Baby to sleep there.

Sleep Training

Many parents are encouraged to "sleep train" (a.k.a. Ferberize) their baby. The idea is that by allowing babies to cry for a little bit longer each night, parents can teach their children to "self-soothe" and "get themselves back to sleep." We are putting these phrases in quotes because as widespread as this notion is, it is a myth.

The big secret that every pediatrician and psychologist knows to be true, but for some reason is reluctant to share with parents, is that infants have no psychological or neurological mechanism that allows them to "self-soothe." A baby's *parasympathetic nervous system* (the part that controls the "calm-down systems" in the brain and body) is not fully developed and will not be for several years. Babies need outside help from Mom and Dad to calm down when they become dysregulated—when baby's heart rate, respiration, and other bodily functions get knocked out of whack by stress. This is true, at least to some degree, even well into toddlerhood.

John Paul II argued in his theology of the body that the human person, at his core, was made most importantly to love and be loved.[29] Science is proving how true this assertion is. Affection from Mom and Dad stimulates the development of the child's *vagus nerve*, the longest nerve in the body, which extends from the brain stem all the way to the gut. It is the vagus nerve's job to reset the body after stress and to help the body come back to a restful, peaceful place after a time of dysregulation. Over time, when parents give babies regular, extravagant affection, babies develop good "vagal tone."[30] Prompt, extravagant affection teaches the vagus nerve to do its job well so that, as the child grows up, he will be more resilient after stress.[31] Good vagal tone has been shown to increase a person's resistance to depression, anxiety, and attention deficit disorders, just as poor vagal tone has been implicated in an increased incidence of these and other emotional disorders.[32]

So if babies can't self-soothe, how does sleep training work? Researchers have found that sleep training works by teaching babies that it is useless to cry when stressed. Sleep-trained babies stop crying, but they continue to exhibit the same level of stress in their bodies (as evidenced by the presence of the stress chemical cortisol) that would be present if they were still crying.[33] In other words, sleep training simply teaches a baby to stop seeking help during distress. Psychologists refer to this state, in which help-seeking behavior is extinguished despite persistent physical signs of stress, as *learned helplessness*. This research shows that babies who are sleep trained will eventually fall back to sleep, but it is not a peaceful slumber as much as it is the exhausted response to knowing that "no one will come when I cry."

At this time, researchers are conflicted about the long-term consequences of sleep training.[34] Some pediatricians argue that the trade-off in better parental sleep is worth the risks that may be associated with sleep training. As of yet, although evidence is building, there are no studies that *conclusively* prove that sleep training is directly associated with lowered ability to respond to stress later in life. However, when we take into account all that is definitively known about baby development, we are very hard pressed to recommend sleep training except in extreme situations where maternal health or marital stability is in question.

Just to summarize: babies develop best when parents give them extravagant amounts of affection, respond promptly to their cries, and keep them as close as possible as much as possible. We also know that there is no known psychological or neurological method by which babies can adequately self-soothe. Add to this the assertions of the theology of the body that our bodies bear witness to the fact that we were not created to be alone, but rather to be part of a loving communion of persons through which we learn—first in our very bones and then in our minds and relationships—to give and receive the extravagant love that comes from God's own heart.

> **Greg:** Having our little ones in our room was a real blessing. There is nothing like waking up to a little one's cuddles and smiles. It's hard to feel bad about your day when you see your child curled up next to your wife looking so peaceful and adorable. I highly recommend it! Some dads I know worry about not being able to sleep if they have the baby in their room. I'm completely sympathetic to that concern—believe me, my clients prefer me well rested. But the most important thing an anxious dad can do is relax. Sleep will come. But those special moments waking up next to your little one are over in what feels like a millisecond. I wouldn't miss that for the world.

> **Lisa:** Practically speaking, I got so much more sleep than the other moms I knew who kept their baby in another room! If our baby fussed, I would just roll over and let the baby nurse, and we'd both fall back to sleep. I was still somewhat tired, of course,

some days more than others. All parents with new babies are tired to at least some degree. There's just no way around that. But I know I would have gone out of my mind if I had had to get up, traipse across the hall, calm the baby down enough to nurse him, nurse him, get him back in his crib, and then try to get myself back to sleep. What a nightmare! Keeping our babies close enabled us to be connected nighttime parents as well as attached daytime parents. At our parish, sometimes we sing a version of Psalm 131 that has the refrain, "Like a child rests in its mother's arms, so will I rest in you." I remember lying there at night, cuddling one of our babies and thinking of that psalm—thinking about how God loved me even more than I loved this little baby. I would imagine God holding me in his arms just the way I held my nursing baby. It made me feel so close to God, so loved by him. I know he loves me, but I really cherish those moments when God lets me feel his presence. Lying there in bed near my baby helped me feel more connected than ever to God's love. If I, with all my faults and selfishness, could love this child so much, how much more did God, who is perfect in every way, cherish me?

Whatever sleeping arrangement you choose, we recommend that you follow your heart and the promptings of the Holy Spirit in responding to your infant's nighttime needs. Respond promptly when your baby cries with as much affection, love, and feeding as the baby needs. Trust the programming God has built into your baby's body and the process of attunement God created in you to teach your baby to regulate her body by listening to yours.

Just Say No to Drama

Nighttime parenting involves some sacrifices no matter how you do it, but we find that those parents who embrace the rhythms and processes God has built into their baby's body enjoy parenting and their children much more than parents who try to impose arbitrary, nonbiologically based expectations, rules, and schedules. The less drama you create around nighttime parenting, the less drama there will be and the quicker everyone will get the rest and the peace of mind they need.

Regardless of how you approach infant sleep, resist the urge to turn tiredness into a catastrophe. While the average person needs about eight hours of sleep to feel *rested*, a person can function normally even if they average only five-and-a-half hours of sleep per day.[35] Therapists who treat sleep disorders point out that people sleep more than they actually think they do because they often confuse lower levels of sleep with wakefulness. Likewise, some research shows that it is anxiety about not getting enough sleep that actually impairs a person's functioning more than the actual lack of sleep.[36]

We aren't trying to minimize the need to be rested. We're just suggesting that it is bad enough to feel tired—you don't need to add unnecessary panic and stress about your sleep on top of it. By all means, do whatever you can to get the sleep you need. Most importantly, sleep when your baby sleeps! As we noted earlier, the littlest babies tend to sleep sixteen hours a day in two- to four-hour stretches. With a little planning, you can get your rest. We include additional tips on getting the rest you need in chapter 5. Just remember the incredibly important advice from that classic parenting tome *The Hitchhiker's Guide to the Galaxy* and "Don't panic!"

As we conclude this section on infant sleep, the words of Mother Teresa are ringing in our ears: "If we have no peace, it is because we have forgotten that we belong to each other." It is hard to think of a context to which these words apply more perfectly than the parent-child relationship both during the day and at night.

Getting Around with Baby

Another thing that can make parenting a newborn more difficult is the sense that it has to be so complicated to leave the house with your baby. If you don't want to feel trapped in your house by parenthood, then we have some great tips that will make baby transport simple.

We are a very mobile couple. We travel a lot for work and pleasure. We go out a lot even when we are at home. When we became parents, we would often look around at other new moms and dads who seemed to need an entire team of Sherpas just to mount an expedition to the grocery store. We find that new parents tend to accidentally make getting around with baby as difficult as it can possibly be by schlepping around more equipment than General Patton brought with him for the Normandy invasion—strollers, playpens, baby carriers, changing mats, bottles, and assorted supplies. We get stressed out just by writing it all down, much less having to lug it.

Keep It Simple

It doesn't have to be that hard. We know it's fun to stock up on all the latest baby gadgets, and all your friends and family— bless their hearts—have been trying to show you how excited they are about your new arrival by buying you every piece of baby equipment known to the modern world. But there is no sense in using it if it doesn't make your life easier.

We regularly hear from new parents both in our counseling practice and on our radio program who are completely stressed about getting around with their newborn. One mom called our show to share how she had to be treated for postpartum depression because she couldn't imagine how she could leave the house by herself with her newborn if she had to drag all the things her baby "needed" with her. While her husband was at work, she ended up trapped in her house feeling completely isolated and overwhelmed at the thought of having to drive to the grocery store. The thought of going to church was panic inducing even with her husband's help. It was just too complicated.

Resist the impulse to make your parenting job harder than it has to be. Getting around with a newborn can be quite easy, especially if you are able and willing to nurse (thereby eliminating all the bottles and formula). All moms really need is a big purse that can double as a diaper bag and a good-quality baby sling. With these two pieces of equipment, the world is at your feet.

> **Greg:** When our first child was six months old, we went on a cruise. Because we know how important bonding time is in the first years of life, we took him along. We got so many shocked and wistful comments from the other passengers on the cruise. "How did you do it?!?" "We could NEVER manage to take all that baby stuff on a plane!" "Oh! I miss our little one so much. I wish we could have brought her!" With our trusty diaper bag and baby sling, we were ready to go.

> **Lisa:** Since I was nursing, he had all the food he needed. When the pressure in the plane started to make his little ears pop, nursing stabilized the pressure in his ears. We had a great time on the cruise itself. He slept in the bed with us so we didn't need a crib and again, nursing was a breeze. We even managed to go to a nightclub act!
>
> That was a little scary. There was a bow-and-arrow act in the show. The climax was this elaborate setup involving a chain reaction of about a dozen crossbows. The star would shoot the first arrow at the first target, which would set off the next

crossbow, which would trigger the next, and so on and so on until the last crossbow shot an apple on top of his assistant's head as she whirled around on a wheel. Up until then the show had been pretty noisy with a lot of music and sound effects. But now, the announcer said, "Maestro, please stop the music! Ladies and gentlemen, for the safety of our performers we must ask you to maintain complete silence during our finale! Please refrain from making *any* noise!"

I looked down at my baby. I thought about making a quick escape from the theater, but I was sitting in a long booth with people on either side of me and I was basically trapped. I had visions of our baby crying out at just the wrong second. The poor woman on the stage was going to be impaled by an arrow, and it was going to be all my fault! Everyone at the table was staring at me. I didn't know what to do. I just let him latch on and nurse and I prayed to God that he wouldn't fuss for the next minute or so. Fortunately, he didn't cry and the woman got to live another day!

Greg: One completely unexpected benefit of bringing our baby on the cruise, though, was that he opened doors for us. Before we left on the trip, Lisa just happened to find a onesie at a local department store that was decorated to look like a tuxedo. It had a little red bow tie and a printed-on tuxedo jacket. We dressed him in it to go to dinner. Well, our waiter thought that was the cutest thing he ever saw. He told the captain about it, and we got an invitation to the captain's table! That was a terrific experience, and we wouldn't have had it unless our baby had come along. Our son's presence also earned us extra-special treatment from the waiter all week; he told us all about his little one at home and made sure we were taken extra-good care of the rest of the cruise. God really blessed that trip.

The point is that getting around with your baby only has to be as hard as you make it. If we can successfully negotiate a life-threatening encounter with crossbows with our kid, you can probably make it to church, or the grocery store, or wherever you need to go with yours.

Put a Sling on 'Em

We like to recommend baby slings over other wearable infant carriers because they are more comfortable and versatile than the other options. If you use wearable carriers that come with metal or plastic frames or only allow you to wear the baby on your chest, you can't change positions if you get tired. With a sling, you can position your baby to face you or face out, and you can adjust the child to almost limitless positions for your comfort and hers. Also, with a little practice, you can move from carrying to nursing effortlessly, and the sling doubles as a great nursing blanket for discreet nursing. Slings are the closest thing your baby will experience to the womb environment, and the gentle rocking allowed by the sling is extremely soothing to your child.[37]

Slings are also relatively inexpensive, so you can get a number of them, either to find the best one for you or to match Mom's various outfits and help her feel a little more put together. Every little thing helps. A basic black sling without batting at the edges was one of our favorites because it was so versatile. It could be easily adjusted to virtually any position, and it went with everything.

Some parents feel a little intimidated trying to figure out how to safely use a sling. After all, when you get it, it just looks like a long piece of cloth with a couple of rings on it. How safe can that be? But it is extremely safe and, to repeat, terrifically versatile. For all the latest ideas on how to best use your baby sling, just search YouTube for various baby sling videos. There are hundreds of instructional videos and they are chock-full of great ideas. Slings can be used much longer than other baby carriers and are a wonderful, comfortable way to keep Baby close well into toddlerhood, making them tremendously cost-effective. (As a side note: to watch the adorable Beyoncé parody "Put a Sling on 'Em," visit http://www.youtube.com /watch?v=PU84rDbdu8Q).

The bottom line is that you don't have to be afraid to leave the house—even by yourself—with your baby. It's possible to do it and be fully present, fun, and fashionable to boot! The idea of venturing forth with Baby can be a little intimidating at first, but if you don't get in your own way either by inventing all sorts of horror scenarios in your head or by feeling like you have to bring the entire Seventh Fleet with you, you'll be out and about with ease and comfort in no time!

Having looked at some basics of newborn care, we share in the next chapter some great ideas that moms and dads need to know to make sure Mom stays healthy and happy during the early weeks and months with Baby. Because it is mostly Mom doing the work of helping baby set his or her neurological and biological rhythms, it's important to put as much energy as possible into helping Mom feel as cared for, content, and confident as possible.

CHAPTER FIVE

Keeping Mama Happy

Mom Care

Taking great care of Mom in the first months is every bit as important as taking exceptional care of Baby. In some ways, it's more important. After all, if Mom is allowed to fall apart, then the whole baby-care system collapses! As the saying goes, "If Mama ain't happy, ain't nobody happy." Trust us, no one wants that.

In this chapter, we offer some important ways moms can take care of themselves and some things dads and others ought to do (and not do) to make Mom's life a whole lot easier By the way, we understand that having a baby is tough on dads too. Research shows that up to 10 percent of dads suffer from postpartum depression.[1] We offer some thoughts for dads in this and later chapters of the book. That said, moms really do deserve special consideration, especially in the first year after Baby is born. Mom's body has been literally stretched to its limits. Her hormones are all over the map. Her shape is constantly changing. Her breasts are probably sore and engorged with milk. She may feel like she is occupying an entirely different body, because she is. It can be wonderful, but it can also be strange and stressful. In the face of all of this change, there is one concern that stands head and shoulders above the rest. *Sleep.* Let's start with addressing what is often the number one concern of new moms and work our way out from there.

Get Sleep

Lisa: If I remember anything about the first six months with our babies it's how absolutely exhausted I felt. I shared briefly earlier in the book that our first was a terrible sleeper. So was our third. I just remember sitting/sprawling on the futon at night with the baby watching the shopping channel because it was the only thing on. I don't know—there was something about seeing other women wearing makeup and being dressed and doing their jobs at four o'clock in the morning that made me think that maybe, somehow, I could do mine. There were three things that helped me survive the tiredness.

First, I made a point to sleep when my baby slept. Too many moms think that baby's naptime is chore time, or Facebook time, or girlfriend time. Using naptime as anything but sleepy time for mama is a mistake. Make taking care of yourself a priority. It's fine to do all those other things if you are at least moderately rested, but if you are exhausted and you are driving yourself to rearrange the spice cabinet or even take out the garbage instead of getting a nap, your priorities could do with some adjusting. For the first six months babies sleep around sixteen hours a day. You need to be sure to get your eight hours in there somewhere. Sure, it will probably be in two-hour bursts, and yes, there will be days when the bags of the bags under your baggy eyes have bags but if you remember to sleep as often as possible when baby sleeps, you will survive.

Second, I worked very hard to take our own advice and not panic. I remember one morning, after a particularly long night, looking at myself and bursting into tears. I honestly wasn't sure how I'd make it until Greg got home. But I took a deep breath, asked God to help me get enough naps to make it, and reminded myself that I was only tired and that it would pass. (Good news, it does!)

Finally, I took full advantage of Greg's willingness to help me get some rest when he came home. I tried hard never to just do the whole "Tag, you're it!" thing because I knew that it wasn't fair to Greg, but more importantly, if I didn't take time to get Greg and the baby reacquainted before I took off, the crying would just keep me up. On the other hand, if I took just ten to fifteen minutes to sit on the floor with Greg and the baby, I could then quietly go off and get some much-needed rest.

Greg: Babies are awesome, but they can also be awesomely hard work no matter how you approach them. Mom and Dad have to be in it together. Was it fun to come home after my second job and nuke myself a frozen dinner while Lisa went off to get a nap? No, of course not. But it's part of the job. And you know what? Once I got past the grumping and refocused on being present to my little one, I remembered what it was all for. I always told Lisa that I was in it for the long haul. Sometimes you have to make short-term sacrifices, but at some point, those sacrifices pay off. At some point, you do get the time you need for yourself, for your marriage, for whatever. You have to be intentional about it. Having those connecting rituals we talked about in chapter 3 really helps, but you just have to work at the task in front of you and try hard to not freak out—at least not too often. If you can do that, then it will all work out. Honest.

Mom, get the sleep you need when you can, how you can. Don't hesitate to ask others to help you get the sleep you need. If you can take care of this one, basic need, everything else will fall into place.

Get Lots of Baby Time

The next tip is a little counterintuitive, but the fact is, the more time you get with your baby, the more peaceful you will feel about your baby. The reverse is also true. The more time you spend away from your baby, the more complicated and potentially stressful your relationship with baby will be. Why?

Remember when we talked about attunement in the last chapter? To recap, attunement is the process by which the baby's body learns to regulate itself and manage stress by synching up with Mom's body rhythms. The baby's brain is still developing at an extremely rapid pace in the early weeks and months after birth, and God designed it to need a model to learn how best to regulate itself. The more skin-to-skin and face-to-face time Baby gets with Mom, the quicker Baby's body learns to synch up with Mom's body and be comforted by Mom's touch, smell, body sounds, and voice.

What about Dad?

Our focus on moms should in no way make you think that Dad's role is somehow less significant or less important. There will be times when Baby definitely prefers and even needs Mom over Dad in the early weeks and months due to the unique prenatal relationship between Mom and Baby. But in no way does that mean that dads are somehow second fiddle or off the hook. The more involved dads are in childcare from day one, the more cared for Mom will feel, the more content in the marriage she will be and the lower her risk of postpartum depression will be.[2] And Baby will benefit as well. The truth is we know that Baby craves a relationship with Dad too!

In fact, the father-baby bond is turning out to be even deeper than most have imagined. The research into the mechanisms of father-infant bonding is still quite new, but advances in brain imaging and other sciences have begun to enable us to see that, more than a psychological bond, an actual physiological connection forms between involved fathers and their infants.[3] Within a few days after birth, fathers experience hormonal changes that make them less aggressive and more nurturing. Animal research shows that male mammals experience brain growth a few days after the birth of pups that enables them to do a better job of recognizing and attending to their pups. These brain regions develop only if the father mammals have physical contact with their pups. Similar animal research shows that the presence of the father is required in order for certain regions of the brain of infant mammals to turn on; these areas simply fail to develop if the father isn't present.

This doesn't apply just to animals. Human research shows that the more involved dads are in childcare from the very first days of their child's life, the more their bodies experience hormonal changes that allow them to be more connected and nurturing to their child. *Interestingly, the highest degree of these hormonally based, nurturance-related changes occurs in men who co-sleep.*[4]

Dad needs to respect the unique nature of the relationship between Baby and Mom, but Dad should feel free to take on all the baby-care tasks his baby is happy to have him do, including comforting. Dad doesn't have the same comforting strategies available to him that Mom does—he can't lactate, for instance—but the low tones of Dad's voice, the sound of his heartbeat, and the different feel of his skin and strong arms all enable Dad to develop a whole different set of comfort strategies that are both unique to him and deeply appreciated by Baby.

A family we know developed a nighttime ritual in which Mom would nurse the baby to sleep and then Dad would gently take the baby and hold him to his chest for twenty minutes or so before bringing the baby to bed, giving Mom some time to wash her face and brush her teeth. While this exact ritual might be disruptive for babies who prefer to nurse directly to sleep and then not be moved, it is an example of how Baby is hardwired to crave his or her own, unique relationship with Dad. When Dad is willing to get involved, Baby learns to respond in kind—and Mom also benefits both practically and emotionally from Dad's loving care of their little one!

The Music of Baby's Life

While Dad's role in childcare is both unique and essential, it should be complementary to Mom's primary role—at least in the first few weeks and months after birth. Some people wonder why it is so important that the baby bond to Mom first. Isn't any loving caregiver sufficient? Let us attempt to address this question with a metaphor.

Imagine, for a moment that you are trying to learn to sing a very complicated song that involves going back and forth from fast to slow and incorporates several key changes over the course of the piece. Now imagine that you are trying to learn this song while ten different people keep coming in and out of the room, and each of them is singing a different tune. What would that experience be like? You might eventually learn the song you needed to learn, but it would be more stressful and more difficult, and you'd probably miss some of the more subtle aspects of the piece. You'd get it done, but it would be much harder than you'd want it to be.

Now imagine that for the entire time you are learning this song, you are working with one partner who patiently hums the melody and the rhythm over and over again. When you miss something, you just have to listen a little bit and there it is again. Learning the song this way might still be hard work, but it wouldn't be stressful, and you would become more confident as you heard the melody over and over and learned to match all its subtlety with perfection.

This is actually a pretty good metaphor for what your baby is trying to do. She is trying to learn the rhythms and melody of her body and how to maintain the melody across many different key changes (environments and moods) so that she can always find her way back to the main melody line (her relaxed state) and avoid going off pitch (becoming dysregulated). When many different caregivers swoop in to try to "give Mom a break," they are like the people in the story who keep coming in the room humming a different song. Their bodies don't sound, feel, and smell like Mommy's body. Their songs are likely good in a different way, but they're still different. They mess up the song Baby is trying to learn, and that can be so frustrating!

The more one-on-one, skin-to-skin, face-to-face time baby gets to spend with Mom, the more easily Baby's body will learn to sing the song of healthy self-regulation and the more in synch Mom and Baby will be. That means less stress for Mom because learning goes both ways. As Baby's body is learning from Mom, Mom is learning to respond, even automatically, to Baby's cues. She begins to learn that this sniffle means "I want to be rocked," and this gurgle means "Feed me, please," and this clucky sound means "My tummy feels funny." Every baby is different, and it takes time to learn your baby's unique language. By getting lots of time with Baby, Mom becomes a "baby whisperer" who learns to decode her baby's special language and is able to respond to the baby's needs often long before the baby gets upset enough to have to cry for help. For almost as long as psychologists have been doing research on infant development, studies have found that the more Baby cries, the more stressed Mom and Dad are. The more one-on-one, skin-to-skin, face-to-face contact Mom and Baby can get, the less stressed both of them will be.

And how does Dad fit into our musical metaphor? Dad represents Baby's first opportunity to learn the harmony to the melody Mom's body has been singing. When Dad is active and present in childcare, working diligently and patiently to develop his own comforting and caring strategies with Baby, his harmony "locks in" the melody Mom's body has been singing to Baby just as a solid harmony locks in the melody in a choir or band. Later, when Baby is confident in his ability to regulate his own bodily systems in the presence of Mom's melody and Dad's complementary harmony, he will also be able to enjoy and integrate the more complicated harmonies and rhythms in the music of other nurturing relatives, friends, and caregivers. But this ability will rest on security Baby has in that basic melody sung by Mom's body and the basic harmony sung by Dad's. Building from this foundation, baby will learn to be a great orchestra conductor, regulating his own bodily systems in the presence of the many different musical styles, rhythms, and syncopations he will encounter as he grows and develops.

We want to be clear that we are not saying that you should never let anyone else hold your child or help care for your baby besides Mom or Dad. Again, there is no need to make life harder on yourself. If you need a nap and your mother-in-law is happy to play with Baby for an hour or so at your house while you get some much-needed rest, by all means take advantage of it. That said, leaving your newborn with someone else for hours at a time *as a habit* is rarely a good idea and tends not to provide the benefits parents are hoping for. When you need a break from Baby, try to get the help to come to your home so that you can be there if Baby needs you.

Get Household Help

If you need a break, there are usually much better things people can do to take care of you than take your baby for extended periods of time. Get over your pride and let other people do anything else they are able to do: laundry, housekeeping, cooking, or running errands. If there is any chore you don't particularly enjoy doing and can pass off to volunteer or paid help, do it. Do it now. You may feel guilty. Don't. There will be some time in the future where you can repay these kindnesses or pay them forward. Please take advantage of the help today.

> **Lisa:** We don't live anywhere near my family. My sister couldn't come out to help at all, but she did offer to pay for a doula for a week. A *doula* is a professional "mom's helper." It's her job to do everything Mom can't do because she's tending to herself and the baby. Honestly, it's probably the sweetest thing she ever did for me. It surely helped me get back on my feet after the baby was born. The doula was only with us for a week, but her presence let me catch my breath, and it really helped to know that even though my family couldn't be there, they were supporting me across the miles.

If you are having a hard time getting the household help you need because you either don't have family near you or can't afford to hire someone, reach out to local parishes or other churches to see if they have a moms' ministry. Many churches provide light housekeeping and other services for new parents. Do you have a college near you? Put up signs offering to trade laundry and home-cooked meals for some light housekeeping and other help.

Again, many people feel guilty accepting help from others, much less seeking it out. Try to remember that in his theology of the body, John Paul II argued that there are two ways we give to each other: first by sharing what we have with them, and second by allowing them to share what they have with us. By becoming receiving givers, we allow others to use their gifts to bless us, and that can be a great source of joy and closeness.[5] Obviously, there are limits, but work with others to figure out what those limits might be. Don't assume you can guess where the lines are all by yourself. Chances are people in your life want to be a lot more generous than you might be giving them credit for!

Take Care of Your Body

Whether you are going to be a full-time stay-at-home mom or you are on maternity leave, those first few weeks and even months postpartum can leave you as tired, hormonal, and probably a little dazed as you are over-the-moon happy with your new little blessing. In light of all this, it can be easy to let "little things" like taking a shower, or getting dressed and brushing your hair, or even eating go by the wayside. Please don't.

> **Lisa:** When I've gotten together with new moms, I've been surprised to witness this weird competition that goes on. I remember one time at a moms' group, a young mother and friend of mine said, "I'm so tired, I couldn't even shower today." Immediately another chimed in with "I don't think I brushed my teeth!" And another mom said, "I don't think I've managed to shower this week yet." It went on like that with each mom chuckling and competing to see who was most exhausted and least able to care for herself. I remember thinking how strange it was. Not that I was spending my days at the spa or something. At the time, I was tandem nursing a two-and-a-half year old and an infant, so I got how hard it can be get a few minutes to take care of one-self. But it was as though these moms were proud of neglecting themselves. They acted like it was a badge of honor that showed how committed they were to motherhood! I don't think a mom shows her commitment to motherhood by actively cultivating a cloud of body odor and bad breath. That's just

working on your martyr card. I think a mom shows her commitment to motherhood by taking care of her baby and maintaining her health so she can continue to take care of her baby.

No one is expecting you to look like a runway model the few weeks after you've given birth—or ever, for that matter. But some basic self-care—a daily shower, a little mascara or lip gloss, and a comfortable but attractive outfit—can do a lot to make you feel like a human being.

Lisa: It was hard remembering the importance of taking care of myself. I have always been pretty tuned in to my kids. I loved spending time with them and meeting their needs, and especially in those early weeks and months, my mind was totally focused on being there for my baby. But thankfully Greg is great about reminding me that if I don't at least get a shower and do some basic maintenance, it's hard for me to feel like I'm not losing it.

Greg: The details will be different in every family, of course, but Lisa and I would try to talk the night before about what she wanted me to do to help her get ready in the morning. Did she need to get up before me to get a shower while I watched the baby and then let her go back to sleep for a while? Did she need to sleep in if possible that morning, but have me set up the baby seat in the bathroom so she could set the baby safely on the other side of the shower curtain when she was getting cleaned up? What could I do to help make sure she could feel at least a little put together every day?

Lisa: Some times were harder than others. Some days Greg would have to head out early, and I would be alone with the baby in the morning. So I'd put the baby in the safety seat Greg had set up for me before he left and I'd get in the shower and play peek-a-boo between soaping up and rinsing. It took a little effort, but honestly it was kind of fun. Our babies often really enjoyed themselves with that game. And if they started to cry, I'd finish up as reasonably quickly as I could, wrap myself in a towel and sit and nurse for a few minutes. That usually restored at least basic order. As for makeup, I wasn't red carpet ready for sure, but I could do a reasonably decent job with some basic makeup while the baby was on my lap, in a sling, or nursing. I also had a few comfortable outfits that I felt good in and made me feel attractive. And though I didn't normally need it, Greg would always offer to iron something for me so I didn't feel like I'd just rolled out of bed.

Greg: My feeling is that providing for my family doesn't just mean bringing home the bacon. I'd have to go to work whether or not I was married. I think it mainly means arranging for whatever needs to happen to make my wife feel loved and cared for and helping create a pleasant, loving environment for my children.

Get the help you need to take care of your basic hygiene and appearance so you can feel competent, confident, and capable of giving your best to your child. Don't be afraid to ask for help from your husband or anyone else you need to assist you in taking care of at least your basic needs.

Help Mom Eat Well

Another aspect of self-care that often takes a hit postpartum is basic nutrition. You may not feel up to cooking anything, so it's easy to just graze on whatever convenience or junk food you have lying around. A cookie for breakfast? Why not? Potato chips for lunch? That'll do. Except that it really won't. New moms need to eat well to keep up their strength and mood. Nursing moms especially need about an extra 500 calories a day just for milk production.[6] And remember, if you're nursing, what you eat, Baby eats.

> **Lisa:** Our cleanup ritual after dinner would include making sure I had something ready for breakfast and lunch the next day. It wasn't anything fancy, but we tried to make sure we had fruit in the house, or that Greg or I made a sandwich to keep in the fridge for the next day's lunch. This way, it was ready when I was hungry. On the days I had more energy, I could make something more for myself if I wanted it, but if I was having a more stressful day, everything would be ready to go. That little bit of preparation went a long way toward making sure I had the energy I needed to keep up with my little one's needs.

Whatever nutritional habits you ultimately develop, being mindful about your eating and preparing a few simple meals the day before when your husband is around can be tremendously helpful for keeping up your strength and your mood.

Avoid "Can't Do It with Baby" Syndrome

Moms are great at doing a number on themselves, especially when it comes to what they think they can and can't do with a baby around. We already mentioned the woman who thought it was impossible to leave the house on her own with her baby. Then there's the mom who wanted to save any significant conversation with her husband until after the baby was asleep because she felt she couldn't concentrate like she wanted to on her husband otherwise. Of course, they never actually got to talk because the baby would either wake up or would have a hard time falling asleep. All of us are tempted to make up

foolish rules that actually prevent us from meeting the very
need the rules were intended to help us meet. Be on the look-
out for yours.

Instead of telling yourself what you *can't* do with baby, ask
yourself, "How *could* I do this with my baby (if I had to)?" For
instance, instead of telling yourself that you can't take a shower
when you are at home by yourself with the baby, ask yourself
how you might keep the baby present and safe while you did.
Perhaps you could set up the playpen outside the shower and
play peek-a-boo. Or perhaps you could ask for suggestions
from more experienced moms who do manage to get clean in
the morning while still attending to their baby. Is this the way
you'd prefer to take care of your hygiene? Probably not. But
that's not the point. Attending to this need—even if you have
to do it under less-than-ideal circumstances—will help you feel
normal, healthy, and empowered, which makes it worth doing
even if you can't do it the way you'd prefer. And after all, this
is not a permanent state of affairs.

Let's try another example. Instead of telling yourself that
you can't focus enough to pray when you are alone with your
baby, ask yourself what shape your prayer time might take
if you prayed with your baby. Perhaps you might kiss your
baby's toes and say, "Thank you, God, for my baby's toes!" and
then kiss her knees and say, "Thank you, God, for my baby's
knees!" and go all the way up, bit by bit, to the top of your
baby's head, wrapping up with a brief prayer asking God to
help you be the mom or dad that your baby needs and giving
a blessing to your child. Again, you can ask more experienced
parents how they do this. Is this the prayer time you're used
to? Probably not. But it is a prayer time that respects and invites
God into your new life as a parent. This is just one example. No
doubt you could come up with many other forms of prayer that
are very meaningful—not in spite of baby, but *because* of baby.

The point is that being new parents gives you a wonderful
opportunity to engage your creativity and flexibility. Babies
require that accommodations be made, but there is very little

that can't be done with a baby around. Women have been picking crops, settling frontiers, working in offices, having conversations, getting chores done, and living full lives with babies in tow from the beginning of time. You can work out whatever you need to do *if* you stop giving yourself "I can't" messages (or listening to other moms and dads who tell you that you can't). You may have to change up how you do things, but at least you can feel that you are still capable of getting things done, which is always invigorating.

Get Help for Postpartum Depression

It is normal to feel tired, emotionally drained, and a little disoriented in the first few weeks after you deliver. This is only natural, considering the wildly fluctuating hormones and changes in your schedule. During this time, many moms experience a general feeling of physical and emotional exhaustion, which is sometimes referred to as the *baby blues*. Assuming a mom is able to get the kind of care we describe in this chapter, the baby blues should resolve without intervention within a few weeks at most.

For about 14 percent of moms, however, this physical and emotional exhaustion hints at a more serious concern known as *postpartum depression,* or PPD.[7] Unlike the baby blues, PPD tends to get *worse* as the weeks and months go by. Moms who are experiencing PPD tend to have a harder time feeling connected to their baby and exhibit many of the following symptoms for at least two weeks:

- Depressed mood that includes tearfulness, hopelessness, and feeling empty inside, with or without severe anxiety

- Loss of pleasure in either all or almost all of your daily activities

- Appetite and weight change—usually a drop in appetite and weight, but sometimes the opposite

- Sleep problems—usually trouble with sleeping, even when your baby is sleeping
- Noticeable change in how you walk and talk—usually restlessness, but sometimes sluggishness
- Extreme fatigue or loss of energy
- Feelings of worthlessness or guilt, with no reasonable cause
- Difficulty concentrating and making decisions
- Thoughts about death or suicide. Some women with PPD have fleeting, frightening thoughts of harming their babies; these thoughts tend to be fearful thoughts rather than urges to harm.

If you have a history of depression or experienced depression during your pregnancy, you may have as much as a 30 percent higher chance of developing PPD. As terrifying as it can be to have PPD, it is nothing to be ashamed of. PPD is not a personal weakness or a failure of mothering, no matter how much a mom may feel like it is. It is an illness that can be successfully treated, especially when you seek treatment early, although it is never too late to get help. Counseling, medication, or both may be needed to help moms get back on track. The good news is that with proper treatment, moms can rediscover their sense of wholeness and happiness and develop the healthy connection with their baby and with motherhood that PPD can threaten. If you suspect that you or a loved one is going through postpartum depression, talk with your ob-gyn about treatment options for you.

Remember the Three Cs

Although there are many other matters of baby and mom care that we just don't have space to address, we hope that the topics we address in this chapter give you the basic sense that you don't have to choose between doing a great job meeting baby's needs and doing a great job meeting your own. *You don't have to choose.* Remember, Catholics believe in the call to serve the common good, and one way to practice this in family life is by making sure that everyone gets their needs met. When needs go unmet, people burn out and become resentful and irritable. Being a new parent is stressful enough without having to bear that burden!

Making sure that both Baby and Mom are getting their needs met—and Dad and the marriage too, for that matter—requires ongoing awareness of the *Three Cs* for success: creativity, consultation, and commitment.

Creativity is the willingness to try new ways to meet your needs even if you're not certain that the new ways are ideal. Creativity keeps you moving forward and allows solutions to evolve naturally over the course of time.

Consultation does not mean reaching out willy-nilly to anyone who has an opinion about how you should parent. Heaven knows there are plenty of those folks lining up. Rather, consultation refers to the willingness to seek counsel from other people whose informed opinions you genuinely respect (to further clarify, not the people you feel you ought to respect or are being pressured by someone to respect, but those whom you *actually respect*). Choose people who will support the parent-child bond God designed you to create. They may or may not include other moms and dads, your extended family, your pediatrician, a trusted counselor, or other people who, in your estimation, have provided not just good advice, but a sane and thoughtful witness to healthy parenting. Be choosy and pick advisors who don't just confirm your biases but challenge you to be a bit more generous than what comes naturally while showing you how not to burn out in the process. That is how family life founded on the sacrament of marriage does its transformative work: by challenging us, day by day, to give a little bit more of ourselves in a way that stretches us without breaking us.

Of course, another aspect of consultation is *prayer*. God is the author of your family, and he has a plan for your lives. God wants to use your family to help you become the generous, loving, peaceful, joyful, faithful person you long to be. He wants to use your efforts to become this person to be an inspiration to other moms and dads who are striving to create the family God has placed on their hearts.

When you're feeling tired, overwhelmed, or confused, instead of rushing headlong into whatever solution immediately presents itself, take a moment to consult with God. Here is an example of a prayer you might use to seek consultation with God when you need a little inspiration:

> Heavenly Father,
> thank you for showering your love
> and your grace on our family.
> Every day you lead us and guide us
> so that we might become people after your own
> heart.
> Lord, we're having a hard time sorting out how
> to meet everyone's needs
> (in such-and-such area of our life).
> Please help us know what your will is.
> Open our hearts and minds to the answers you
> have in store.
> We love you, Lord. Let your love rule our lives.
> Amen.

Of course, you should feel free to use your own words. This was just one idea to get you started. Talk to God throughout your day. Seek his guidance and be confident in his leadership. When you and your house seek to serve the Lord (Jo 24:15), he will show you how to create a family life that makes you wake up each morning rejoicing in the work God is doing in your life and in your home.

> Then you shall call, and the LORD will answer,
> You shall cry for help, and he will say: "Here I am!"
> —ISAIAH 58:9

Commitment means that if at first you don't succeed—or if at first you don't succeed as well as you would like—you must keep trying. Creating the unique family life God wants to give you is a work in progress. Once you make a plan, keep revisiting and revising it until it really works for you. Discovering the plan that works for you might take time, but if you keep an open heart and mind and remember the Three Cs of creativity, consultation, and commitment, you will be surprised at how God will work with you to create the truly loving, joyful family of your dreams.

CHAPTER SIX

Growing Closer

Marriage Care

Our Catholic faith tells us that children are a gift from the Lord and that having children gives parents an opportunity to grow even closer to each other in the family school of love.[1]

We know that a lot of parents roll their eyes at this. Conventional wisdom, and even some research, suggests that once children come on the scene, marriage is doomed.[2] Then again, another study shows not only that the birth of children makes couples happier, but that the more kids a couple have, the happier they are![3]

Obviously there is more to the story. It turns out that how a couple handles the birth of their children is what spells the difference between postpartum marital bliss and marital diss! In this chapter, we show you how to make sure you are among those couples whose marriage improves with children—just like our faith says it can.

Jake and Carrie Ann

Jake and Carrie Ann are the proud parents of Elise, a happy four-week-old baby girl. Everyone is doing really well in general, but Jake and Carrie Ann have been experiencing some tension in their marriage.

"It's just been really hard balancing everything," says Jake. "I think we're doing a pretty good job with work and the house and the baby, but I just feel like our relationship is getting lost in the shuffle. We used to make time to talk in the evenings but Carrie Ann's so tired these days, and we aren't getting that time to connect. We haven't been on a date since Elise was born and, of course, Carrie Ann isn't anywhere near ready to resume our sex life. As happy as I am about being a dad is as nervous as I feel that I'm losing my best friend."

"And I just feel pressured and like I'm letting him down," says Carrie Ann. "I'm really doing the best I can being there for Elise and Jake—never mind me—but I'm just so tired. I feel like I should be back to normal by now. I see these moms on TV and in the magazines who are back to pre-baby weight and running around, and I'm just nowhere near any of that. I love Jake, but I just don't have it in me to be there the way I used to be, so I feel like I'm disappointing him. Then I get resentful. I never thought I'd feel this way, but around the edges, I've caught myself thinking of him like he's another kid that needs my attention, and I just want to yell, 'Please, will you just grow up!' I know that's not right. I don't want to feel that way, but there it is."

"I'm picking up on that big time," says Jake. "I'm not trying to put pressure on her. I keep thinking that taking time for our relationship would be good for both of us but somehow it keeps getting turned around like I'm making it about 'me.' I don't get that. It really hurts my feelings. I asked her the other day about getting my mom to watch Elise so we could go out to dinner. I thought Carrie Ann would like a night out to get away. She got upset! I'm not trying to make this about me, but I'm not sure how to remind her that we'll both feel better individually if we take care of us."

"I did get upset about the date thing, and I feel bad about that," says Carrie Ann. "But I just feel like Jake doesn't get it. Of course I love him. Of course I want to spend time with him, but the date idea was just not gonna work for me. In the first place, I just don't feel comfortable leaving the baby already. I'm nursing, and that relationship is really important. Sure, I could pump, but then if my milk dries up from not nursing for a couple of hours, I would be really sad. I just don't want to take that chance right now. I know he thinks I'm crazy for that, but that's where I'm at and I wish he could understand. And second, I'm just too exhausted to even think about getting ready to go out to a fancy restaurant. I'm still really uncomfortable. I mean, I'm getting out and doing what I have to do, but the thought of putting on all my makeup and doing my hair and getting on a pretty dress and heels just makes me feel so overwhelmed. I'm not even sure I have something that fits, and I just don't need the torment of going through my closet right now. God help me, I know I should have been grateful that he wanted to take me out, but I just wanted to rip his face off! What's wrong with me?"

There isn't anything seriously wrong with Jake and Carrie Ann. Their experience is pretty normal. Even so, it can feel a little disturbing if you didn't know what to expect. Here's the good news. Jake and Carrie Ann's marriage isn't falling apart. They're just in transition. The things they used to do to try to connect aren't working anymore. They can and—with a little *creativity, consultation,* and *commitment*—will discover new ways to connect eventually, but right now, rather than engaging the creativity we discussed in the last chapter, Jake and Carrie Ann are clinging to the old ways of connecting: talking in the evening, going on date nights. Unfortunately, those things just aren't going to work the same way right now. They might work again at some point in the future, but right now, Jake and Carrie Ann need some new ideas. In this chapter, we look at some ideas for taking great care of your marriage once your baby arrives on the scene.

The Marriage Dynamic with Baby Added In

The first thing to look at is the marriage dynamic. As we noted in our book *Just Married: The Catholic Guide to Surviving and Thriving in the First Five Years of Marriage*, the wife tends to be the relationship caretaker during the early, prebaby years in lot of marriages. It is often the wife who reminds her husband about the importance of making time to talk, or pray, or see friends, or have a date.[4]

Once Baby comes along, the wife's attention is drawn to the very important work of bonding with Baby. Hopefully by now, based both upon our discussions and your personal experience, you realize that strong bonding and attachment doesn't just happen. It takes real effort. Because of this new responsibility, however, the wife no longer has the time or energy to be the relationship caretaker—at least not to the same degree as before. At this point, one of two things can happen.

Option 1: Loneliness and Baby-Phobia

The first possibility is that the husband will expect things to stay as they were. Assuming that his wife will maintain her role as relationship caretaker, he just waits for her to start taking care of things again. He may experience feelings of jealousy toward the baby and become somewhat withdrawn. In turn, his wife will become resentful as she comes to see him as "another kid" she has to attend to. Depending on how things play out, the couple could recover as the baby gets older and the wife can resume her relationship caretaking role (although such a couple would probably be somewhat baby-phobic in the future), or this could be the beginning of the end of the romantic relationship altogether as the wife loses herself in taking care of the children and the husband further distances himself, assuming that "this is just the way it is" once you start having kids.

Option 2: Deeper Intimacy

The second option is much more hopeful and rewarding. In this scenario, the husband makes it his job to take as good care of his wife as she takes care of the baby. He works hard to ask her what she needs and to follow through on her requests. He also keeps his eyes open so that he can try his best to anticipate needs that she may not be able to express. He doesn't impose his agenda on her (e.g., you MUST go on a date night with me; you MUST give my mom the baby and get out to do something for yourself). He realizes that, in these early months, *Mom is nesting* with her baby. Well-intentioned though they may be, ideas for creating marital connection or providing mom care that tear Mom out of the nest or even *potentially* put distance between Mom and baby can automatically feel threatening or, at the very least, undesirable. Remember, especially during these early weeks and months, baby's brain and bodily systems are synching up with Mom's brain and bodily rhythms—that's the physiological component of attachment and bonding. If a mom is properly bonded, leaving baby at this stage often feels physically threatening. A mom can be pushed to ignore this feeling, but she'll usually resent it; and even if you can get her to do what she is being asked, it rarely pays off the way the couple hopes it will. Therefore, strategies for connection and mom care have to respect the nesting/bonding instinct.

Time to Revisit Those Connecting Rituals

This is where the importance of the rituals for work, play, talk, and prayer, which we discussed in chapter 3, shows itself. If you had these rituals well established before and throughout the pregnancy, then chances are you are in a pretty good place regarding your confidence in the relationship and your level of rapport. You are used to being intentional about them, so making an effort in this area will feel normal.

If you haven't created those connecting rituals before Baby, then you may have a little more work to do because you just aren't as used to being intentional about these activities. They "just happened" before, and now it's going to take more effort. That's okay. Just know that this is a normal transition and that any growing pains you feel (in the form of some disconnection from your spouse or concern about the relationship) are normal. How quickly those feelings pass will depend upon how hard and intentionally you work to establish those connecting rituals now.

If you already have well-established connecting rituals for work, play, talk, and prayer, take time to revisit those. Chances are, many of the habits you cultivated around these rituals won't work now or won't work as easily. That's not to say that they might not work again at some point in the future, but you may need to identify simpler variations for this new phase of your marriage.

For instance, if you used to take a weekly date night out every Friday evening, perhaps for the next several months, you will want to have a date night *in*. Get takeout from your favorite restaurant or make a nice meal. Bring out the good plates. Light candles. Create a romantic music channel on your Internet radio app. Present a small gift (e.g., a card with a poem, flowers, a small charm for a bracelet, or a note that lists all the things you love about your spouse). Even a couple on the tightest budget can write a love note or do something thoughtful for each other. Sure, the date's at home, but it can still be special. Be creative. Again, the husband can take charge of this. Sweep her off her feet. Use this time to make her feel 100 percent loved and cared for. Your efforts will show her that you are the man she can lean on and find her strength in, instead of one more responsibility to attend to.

Here are a few more examples. Perhaps you used to have a work ritual around gardening, but Mom isn't feeling very much like squatting in the dirt these days. Perhaps your new work ritual could be bathing your baby together! This was something we did, and it was great fun watching our baby interact with the water and discover his fingers and toes. It was a great time for light conversation too!

If you used to take time to talk after dinner, but your baby is fussy at this time, perhaps you will want to take time to talk while the baby is nursing. Remember what we wrote in the last chapter about avoiding arbitrary rules that make your life harder. Everything we said about such rules when it comes to mom care applies twice as much to relationship care. Too many couples fall into all-or-nothing thinking when it comes to meeting their couple needs: "If we can't get date time, talk time, prayer time, or project time the way we want to get it, the way we used to get it, or the ideal way we'd prefer to get it, then we just won't get it." This is a profoundly foolish attitude that leads to marital breakdown and resentment toward parenthood. The important thing at this stage is getting the needs for work, play, talk, and prayer met in any way you can and maintaining your connections across these important categories. You can always improve on these rituals and get more out of them later on. For now, with a new baby, count merely making them happen relatively consistently a huge success that will benefit your marriage and budding family for years to come.

Date Night Out with Baby

This is probably a good place to talk about "time out." Not the punishment—we mean going out together for dates or other special time. We are a couple who loves going out to the park, to dinner, to movies and plays. Once we had babies, especially little ones we didn't think were ready to be left, it was more difficult to do some of these things. It was not, however, impossible, and with a little creativity, you too can make it work. The following are some best practices for going out with Baby.

Sit Near the Exit

You CAN go to movies and even live performances with Baby. We once took a two-and-a-half-year-old and a three-month-old to a traveling production of *The Lion King*. Lisa ended up seeing a lot of it through the window in the outside door while I kept the toddler happy, but we managed to enjoy ourselves anyway. That said, if you are going to attempt such a daring feat, sit near an exit so that you can bug out if the baby begins to fuss *at all* (please don't inflict a fussing baby on your neighbors). If you do have to step out, a baby sling comes in really handy. Put the baby in the sling and try to nurse the little one down. Then, adjust the sling so that the baby is resting just above your lap and return to your seat. When you sit back down, because the sling is adjusted, the baby won't jostle around and won't really feel the difference between your sitting and standing. She will continue to feel like she is suspended in the sling. This same process works for movie theaters and restaurants.

Ask for a To-Go Box with Your Meal

You CAN go to restaurants with your baby, and the sit-by-the-exit rule works well in these situations. But sometimes your little one won't settle no matter what. That's why, when you go to a restaurant, you should always order to-go boxes at the same time you order your meals. Also, keep meals simpler. Try to limit dinner to an hour or so, max. Stick to entrees and desserts (or appetizer and entree if you don't have a sweet tooth). If you've tried to soothe the little one several times by stepping out but the baby is inconsolable, have Mom head out to the car. Dad can scoop everything into the to-go boxes and settle up with the server. Then, at home, Dad can get out the nice plates and candles. Finish up dinner at home. Is it as good as going out by yourselves? No. It's better. Because now, you not only get dinner, you get an adventure! Have an adventurous spirit, and you'll collect funny stories to tell as well as great meals.

> **Greg:** We went out to dinner for our anniversary when our first was five months old. It was . . . tricky. He was having a tough time that night, and no matter what we did, he just wouldn't stay calm. Lisa tried to nurse him discreetly at the table, and when that didn't work, she took him out to the lobby. He would settle out there, but as soon as she brought him back to the table, he'd start to fuss again.

> **Lisa:** It was quite unusual, because we'd been out to restaurants with him several times before and it went just fine. It all worked out though. I just went to the car and Greg got everything in to-go boxes. We took it all home, and while I settled the baby, Greg got out the good dishes and candles and we celebrated at home. Some people might think it was stressful, I guess, but for us, it was a chance worth taking. If we had been able to stay out, it would have been a great night out. As it was, it made us feel good to work together to save the night. And it's worth it to try not to feel trapped just because you have a baby. As long as you can just roll with things, everything can work out great.

Bring Quiet Activities for Baby

Chances are, the youngest baby will be happy just to sit in
your lap and occasionally nurse, but even so and certainly for
slightly older babes, you'll want to bring some quiet (and we
do mean quiet), soft activities/distractions for Baby. Soft books
with lots of textures are ideal, as are a few little plush animals.
Don't pack the whole menagerie—just a few little distractions
to get you through dinner are enough. But again, please make
sure they are quiet distractions. A beeping iPhone app is not
a lot less irritating to the strangers around you than a crying
baby. You don't have to be a prisoner in your own home, but
you do have to be polite.

Go to a Few Favorite Places Repeatedly

If you go out to the same two or three restaurants or other
places again and again, the staff will get to know you. They'll
see that you are good, attentive parents who don't scare
away customers, and they'll be so happy for your example
that they'll treat you like royalty. We can't tell you how many
free desserts and other complimentary bonuses we've gotten
from waitresses who fell in love with our babies. If they see
you being attentive to your child and thoughtful of their other
guests, the staff and management of your favorite places will
be ready for whatever unusual requests you might have to
keep Baby happy while you get your night out.

Expect an Adventure

If you go out for a date night with your baby, some would say
you're asking for trouble. As we suggested previously, we think
you're looking for adventure. If you dress your baby up, use
the best practices we're recommending here, and go with the
mindset that you may have to leave at a moment's notice, you
can still pull off a night out more often than not. Likewise, if you
are careful not to subject the other patrons in the room to more

than a *little*, barely audible fussing, you will get TONS of praise for having the guts to take your baby where no one else had the courage to go. Again, we are not encouraging parents to inflict their screaming children on patrons of the arts and restaurants who paid good money for a quiet and enjoyable night out. We are not the militant, "I defy you to tell me that my baby's wails are not music" type. But as long as you carefully attend to your child, are sensitive (but not hyper-anxious) about the other people in the room, and are ready to go with your backup plan if necessary, we guarantee that not only will you manage to have more successful nights out than not, but you will be a witness to others that babies do not have to be a prison sentence.

Why Not Just Get a Sitter?

Some people reading this will ask why you would not just get a sitter. We've two thoughts on this question. In the first place, not every family has access to trusted childcare or the money to pay for a sitter. We are of the mindset that we wouldn't give our baby to anyone we wouldn't trust with our credit card and PIN number. That limits things a bit, but we feel our children are worth the sacrifice.

Second, most babies are simply not ready to be left even for an hour or so for at least the first several months. Yes, many parents do it, but that doesn't mean it's a great idea for the bonding process. Remember, until toddlerhood a baby really doesn't understand that he isn't still a part of Mom—after all, he was literally part of Mom's body for nine months. The baby doesn't even begin to consider that he might be separate from Mom until at least five months. Until then, when Mom goes away, the child feels as if a part of him is missing.

Keep in mind that *individuation* (the process by which the baby learns she is separate from Mom) is a process. It does not happen at six months. It *begins* about then and continues to unfold in varying degrees until around twenty-four months, when the baby's brain has developed to the point that she can imagine that Mommy still exists even when she can't see or hear her. Before that, Mommy's not being there is a distressing event. Do babies handle separations before this age without bursting into flames? Of course. Just like you would survive if you started seeing your right arm appearing and disappearing at random. But that doesn't mean that making a habit of regular separations is a good idea. Remember, *a calm baby is a learning, developing, maturing baby.* The more stressed your baby becomes—and nothing is more stressful to the newborn than separation—the more she may tend to lag with attachment and achieving developmental milestones. Most children tend to catch up eventually, but why put your baby (and yourself) through struggles if you don't have to?

As your child is learning that he is a separate person from Mommy, he can usually tolerate short separations. Use your relationship with your child to know how long your child can handle being away from you. Usually, by five or six months, a child can handle being separate from Mom for about an hour or so if he is cared for by an attentive caregiver and Mom gives him a little extra time to reconnect upon her return. Babies are not accessories that can be picked up and put down at will. You have to mind your connection with them and, when you are away for even a short time, attend to reconnecting.

What about Sex?

For husbands in particular, the postpartum moratorium on sexual intimacy can be a challenge. We say "for husbands" not because wives don't enjoy sex, but because wives are physically compromised after delivery. To put this in perspective for the dads reading this, without too much exaggeration, passing a baby through the vaginal canal is roughly equivalent to passing a soccer ball though the penis. Men, in all honesty, if you were to accomplish such a heroic feat, would six weeks be a long enough recovery for you to return to full sexual functioning? Exactly.

The reality is that despite what moms read in celebrity news, it takes about a year—with effort—for a mom to completely heal and return to approximately her prebaby body. But that doesn't mean that a couple has to avoid sex for a year after baby. Not at all!

What it does mean is that it is unrealistic for anyone to think that just because the ob-gyn says that Mom is cleared for the resumption of sexual relations by about six weeks or so, everything is ready to go back to "business as usual." Try to remain sensitive to the fact that there is still a lot of healing going on. The following are some suggestions to help get your sexual relationship back on track in the first months postpartum.

Don't Make Sex about Proving the Relationship Is Okay

Many couples look to their sexual relationship to affirm that the relationship is strong and the couple is connected. This is a mistake. While a vital sexual relationship is an important part of marital satisfaction, the more important parts have to do with the maintenance of their connecting rituals. If a couple has strong connections through work, play, talk, and prayer and works hard to maintain those connections in the first weeks and months post-delivery, they will be in a much better position to handle postpartum sexual abstinence. It still might not be easy, but it will be manageable because the husband and wife are finding important ways to hold on to each other despite either the lack of a sexual connection or, once intercourse is renewed, the tentative nature of that connection. Stay away from the temptation to feel that you need to prove anything to each other right now. Have confidence that the baby you have cocreated with God is a sign that you share a love so powerful that it has taken on physical form. Of course, you still need to take care of your relationship, but relax and give each other some credit for now. Work consistently on finding ways to connect via work, play, talk, and prayer; and know that your physical relationship will come back on line once some healing occurs and energy is restored.

Foreplay Is Important

When resuming sexual relations it will be important to proceed slowly and gently. Likewise, take your time with plenty of foreplay. Helping each other—and especially the wife—relax and feel cared for is terrifically important, not just psychologically but physiologically as well. Kissing, cuddling, massaging, and direct but gentle manual or oral stimulation of the genitals (which is permissible to Catholics so long as it does not continue to climax) helps to loosen and lubricate the vaginal walls—two things that are very important for avoiding painful intercourse. The more time you take leading up to penetration, the more pleasant the experience will be for the both of you. That might seem counterintuitive if you are afraid that Baby could wake up at any second, but resist the temptation to rush. Better to have some interrupted intimate time together that makes you want more time with each other than rushed, unpleasant or painful sex that makes at least one of you want to avoid it altogether.

Let the Woman Take the Lead

At least for the first few times you are trying to be physically intimate after the birth of your baby, it's probably best if you rely on positions that allow the woman to dictate the depth and speed of penetration. Since she knows what feels good to her and what doesn't, it's a good idea to let the wife decide what works best for her. This eliminates the guesswork for the husband and increases the likelihood that lovemaking will be enjoyable for both of you. For more tips on how to get the most out of your post-baby sexual life, check out our book *Holy Sex!: A Catholic Guide to Toe-Curling, Mind-Blowing, Infallible Loving*.[5]

Dad's On Point

Before we close this chapter with an exercise to help facilitate your discussion about how you might need to adapt your connecting rituals, we want to remind Dad that, ideally, you are the man to make these things happen. Of course your wife should be involved in the planning as much as she is able to be, but if you make it your job to generate three or four options and do the legwork to make those options possible, then you can get her feedback on which option works best for her, or if she'd prefer something else altogether. If she would like to be more involved, that's terrific. We highly encourage it. But the point is that she should feel like she doesn't have to do it unless she has the energy for it. Dad, your taking responsibility for generating ideas for maintaining connection that respect her need to bond with Baby frees her up to see you as her knight in shining armor—the strong man who protects her from everything that threatens her ability to connect with Baby. It gives her a shelter (your secure relationship) in which to feel refreshed and recharged, and reminds her (without pressuring her) that she is more than "just a mom." If you follow the suggestions in this chapter, Dad, you will support the process that allows a couple to grow closer together because of Baby instead of becoming another one of those couples who think marriages die once children come on the scene.

Keeping It Close to Home: An Exercise

When you have a new baby, it is important to use the three Cs of creativity, consultation, and commitment to adapt those important rituals you've established for staying connected as husband and wife through work, play, talk, and prayer—even while keeping close to Baby. Although in the early years of marriage it can be wonderful to get out of the house to go on dates and other excursions, for the next few months, you might need to adjust your rituals to respect your family's need to be together, bond, and perhaps stay home.

Maintaining and Adapting Your Rituals

The following exercise gives you an opportunity to creatively adapt your existing connecting rituals to your new reality as parents. In the first space under each heading, write down examples of things you used to do regularly to maintain that part of your relationship. In the second space, write down how you might adapt those rituals so that you could do them at home and with a baby around. It isn't as impossible as you might think at first. We've given several practical examples throughout the chapter of what this can look like. Just be creative, consult with your spouse and other couples for ideas, and remain committed to the belief that you can meet your needs as a couple *and* meet your baby's attachment needs.

Working Together Rituals

Here are some ways my spouse and I used to work together before we had our baby.

(Example: We used to garden together.)

_____

_____

_____

Now, look at the above ideas. How might you change or adapt them so that they (or something similar) could be done safely and enjoyably at home with a baby around? Be creative. In fact, don't be afraid to be a little silly. You're just brainstorming. You can fine-tune your thoughts later.

Here are some new ways we can work together now that we have a baby.

(Example: We can bathe the baby together).

_____

_____

Playing Together Rituals

Here are some ways my spouse and I had fun together before we had our baby.

(Example: We used to go out to dinner every Friday.)

_____

_____

_____

Now, look at the above ideas. How might you change or adapt them so that they (or something similar) could be done safely and enjoyably at home with a baby around?

Here are some new ways we can have fun together now that we have a baby.

(Example: Every Friday night, we can order takeout from our favorite restaurants and serve it on our good china with candles in the dining room.)

_____

_____

_____

Talking Together Rituals

Here are some ways my spouse and I used to get time to talk together before we had our baby.

(Example: We used to take a walk after dinner.)

_____

_____

_____

_____

How might you change or adapt these now that Baby has joined you?

Here are some new ways we can get time to talk together now that we have a baby.

(Example: We can make a point of talking during baby's nursing time in the evening.)

_____

_____

_____

Praying Together Rituals

Here are some ways my spouse and I used to pray together before we had our baby.

(Example: We used to pray together before bed each night.)

_____

_____

_____

_____

Now, look at the above ideas. How might you change or adapt these?

Here are some new ways we can pray together now that we have a baby.

(Example: Every night, we'll give the baby a blessing and pray for whatever concerns our family has.)

_____

_____

_____

The Honey-Care List

Dads, remember: having a great marriage after you bring
the baby home involves taking as good care of your wife
as she is taking care of the baby. Write down as many
special little things your wife has asked for or seemed to
appreciate when you did them for her in the past (e.g.,
get flowers, look at her when she's talking to you, wash
the dishes, give her a big hug, etc.) as you can. Try to
identify at least twenty-five ways to cherish your wife
based on your observation and what she's told you. Of
course, if you're not sure, by all means ask her. Each day,
do at least two things on the list. Try to do two different
things every day.

1. _____

2. _____

3. _____

4. _____

5. _____

6. _____

7. _____

8. _____

9. _____

10. _____

11. _____

12. _____

13. _____

14. _____

15. _____

16. _____

17. _____

18. _____

19. _____

20. _____

21. _____

22. _____

23. _____

24. _____

25. _____

Integrating Baby into Your Life

Throughout this chapter, we've looked at ways the most successful couples handle the transition to parenthood while maintaining a healthy marriage. To summarize, successful couples do not set marriage and parenting in competition with each other. Instead, they acknowledge that everyone has needs and has a right to have those needs met, and they try to creatively attend to everyone's needs as much as is possible. Couples who manage this transition best tend to be couples where Mom focuses on baby bonding and Dad attends to both Mom's and the marriage's well-being in the most baby-friendly way possible. When dads take a baby-friendly approach to mom and marriage care, they avoid stressing out Mom and Baby and causing their well-intentioned efforts to backfire.

The fact is that babies do change things. But remember, it is how you view your children that determines whether the changes cause you to fall more in love with each other or become stressed and strained. If you cling to rigid ideas about what it means to be a couple and what babies "should" be able to do (versus what your baby is actually capable of doing), you will probably have a stressful time of it. If, on the other hand, you are flexible and creative about the ways you can connect as a couple and make sure to connect in a way that welcomes both your baby and your baby's actual needs and personality, you'll do great.

The Church teaches that babies are a gift from the Lord and that couples and families should grow closer together because of the presence of children. Research bears this assertion out. Couples who follow the advice we've offered in this chapter will be equipped to live the ideal of family life that the Church proclaims is the vision God holds for you. You will be stretched. You'll have to work a bit, and some days will admittedly be tougher than others, but we promise you—based both on our personal experience and on the experience of hundreds and hundreds of young families we've worked with—you will be pleased with the results.

CHAPTER SEVEN

The Spiritual Life of Your Newborn

It might seem a little strange, at first, to talk about the spiritual life of newborns, but can any new parent really doubt that God is working in profound and deeply moving ways through the little ones he gives us? We believe that God moves mightily through our babies. He calls us closer to him through them and he asks us to prepare them to know him, who is the source of the joy that bubbles up from inside of them.

> **Chiara:** Being a mom is such an incredibly spiritual experience. My son is so innocent, so precious, so . . . amazing! Maybe it's silly, but I just feel so close to God when I hold our baby and look at him. Nothing in this broken world could make something as perfect as my baby. He's the best sign to me that God exists and that he loves me. I just sort of marvel when I look at him.

> **Franklin:** I love holding my little girl. I know it's silly to say this, but it seems like she sees so much more than I do. Like she's just more aware. Everything is so new and exciting. I love discovering the world

again through her eyes. Life just seems so much more meaningful since she's come into the world.

Many people believe that to become a saint, one has to head out to far-off lands and do great things for the kingdom of God. The truth is that it is sufficient, as Mother Teresa famously said, to "do small things with great love." However, there are two major spiritual undertakings that new parents should be aware of from birth to six months: laying your child's spiritual and moral framework and preparing for Baptism.

Laying Your Child's Spiritual and Moral Framework

> With my own voice I will call out to the
> LORD, and he will answer me from his holy
> mountain.
>
> —PSALM 3:5

> Whatever you did for one of these least
> brothers of mine, you did for me.
>
> —MATTHEW 25:40

Faith, in purely psychological terms, is the ability to believe— even beyond reason—that something outside of you exists; can give meaning to your life; and, even more remarkably, wants to make things work for your good. Children begin learning faith lessons long before they have language or even the ability to reason. The analyst Erik Erikson argued that *basic trust*, the gut-level understanding that when I call out, someone will answer me, is the first and most important developmental task. Emory University psychologist Dr. James Fowler identified what he called *stages of faith*, which begin with the establishment of basic trust in infancy.[1] Essentially, we know that a child's ability to develop this gut-level trust translates directly into the degree to which a child will eventually express the ability to trust in God.

Have you looked at the world lately? Where in heaven's name does faith—trust in God—come from? It comes to us as a gift. That little seed of faith is planted in us by God. But that seed must be watered and nurtured by Mom and Dad if it is to flower and bloom. This is exactly what Mom and Dad are doing when Baby cries out and they respond promptly to those cries. Or better still, when parents and Baby are so attuned to one another that Mom and Dad know, even before the cries come, that this gurgle means "I'm hungry" or that snuffle means "I need to be changed." In Isaiah 65:24 God promises his children, "Before they call, I will answer; while they are yet speaking, I will hear." This is the God we must prepare our children to trust! Our prompt attention teaches our children that this God exists; before they can begin to conceive of him intellectually, they know the God of love in their bones.

Have you ever had the experience of trying to "leave something at God's feet" (i.e., trying to give a concern to God and then not worry about it because you trust that he will take care of it) only to have that same concern come back to haunt you again and again? You have intellectually entrusted that concern to God, but on that deeper, gut level, you are afraid to trust. Everyone feels this fear, but not everyone feels it to the same degree. Psychologists who study faith development argue that an infant's experience of the consistency of parental response and the time lag between their crying out and a parent's response predicts that child's later ability to intentionally trust God without trying to claw the problem back out of God's hands.[2]

You are giving your child religious instruction each time you put that baby to your breast, each time you pick him up, each time you respond to his cries, each time you hold him close. Each thing you do that says, "You can trust me. Before you call, I will answer; while you are yet speaking, I will hear," teaches your child that there is a God who loves her and wants her to place her trust in him. The faith lessons you teach at this level cannot be taught intellectually and cannot be untaught later on. They can be built upon and mediated by life experience but not deconstructed. Like all the other lessons your child is learning about life and relationship, these lessons are foundational and permanent because they are preverbal, neurologically hardwired, and experienced on a preconscious, gut level.

Parental Response and Moral Development

More fascinating still, the work of developmental psychologists like University of Notre Dame's Dr. Darcia Narvaez shows that prompt parental attention to cries in infancy wires the moral reasoning centers of the child's brain and establishes the child's ability to make quick moral decisions under pressure later on in life.[3]

Have you ever wondered why it is possible to know the right thing to do but still find it almost impossible to do that thing when the pressure is on? Making moral decisions under pressure requires that very different and distant parts of your brain communicate with each other and come to conclusions in a millisecond. How capable a person is of doing the right thing under pressure depends greatly—though perhaps not exclusively—on whether the neural pathways connecting these disparate parts of the brain are donkey trails or superhighways. What determines whether a brain's "moral highways" are hiking trails or the autobahn? Early data strongly suggests that the answer is the amount of parental affection a child experiences in the early months and years of life. Brain researchers know, for example, that affection plays a significant role in facilitating a process called *myelination*.[4] Myelin is the fatty coating around our nerve cells that acts like the rubber insulation around an electrical wire. Myelin sheathing enables electrical impulses in the brain to travel from point A to point B thousands of times faster than they can along less well myelinated pathways. When we give our babies extravagant affection, respond promptly to their cries, feed them upon request, and keep them close to us, we provide all the supplies the brain's "road construction crew" needs to build the superhighways that connect all the moral and relationship centers of the babies' developing brains.

In a particularly fascinating study, researchers examined five hundred children over the course of thirty years and found that the amount of affection a participant was given as a toddler predicted that participant's ability to make good moral choices, demonstrate empathy for others, and have rewarding relationships as a thirty-year-old![5] We discuss this dimension of moral development at much greater length in our book *Beyond the Birds and the Bees: Raising Sexually Whole and Holy Children.*[6]

The point is that at this stage, parents are teaching their baby's brain how to think and feel about other people and the world at large. Parents' responses to Baby lay down neural patterns that serve as the deepest foundation for later lessons that will be conveyed by language and intentional practice. These neural patterns will either provide the child with a deep sense of trust, belonging, and security no matter what the world throws at him later, or they will cause him to feel a deep sense of distrust, isolation, and insecurity even if his world ends up being safe and healthy.[7]

> **Lisa:** As miraculous and exhilarating as the early days of parenting are, they are often also exhausting and intimidating. But knowing the foundation I was laying down for my children always helped me plug into God's grace and trust that he was giving me all I needed to rise to the occasion. So many moms think of themselves as "just a mom." I thank God every day that I know the value of the work that I do. I know that because I am present to my children, I am carving channels into my children's minds and souls to receive the grace he wishes to pour out over them. The work I do as a mom will

determine whether those channels are tiny scratches on the pavement of their brains or deep canyons. I am committed to doing everything I can to help my children be open to all the grace God wants to give them. No one could ever tell me that I could do anything more important than that with my life.

Family Prayer

In addition to the preverbal, neurologically based spiritual and moral training you are giving your baby in the way you care for her, now is a great time to begin family prayer if you have not already been doing it.

You might think that it is silly to begin praying with your baby before she can understand what's going on, but consider all the other things you do with your baby even though he or she doesn't understand. You talk to your baby even though she can't talk. In fact, talking to your baby teaches her language. You play with your baby even though she doesn't understand the rules of any games. In fact, playing with your baby teaches her to interact and play. In the same way, praying with your baby is the best way to establish the early patterns that make talking and relating with God an integral part of your family life and an integral part of your child's makeup. Are we suggesting sticking a rosary into your baby's hands and propping her up in a kneeling posture? Of course not! But we are suggesting introducing your baby to God in little ways that will bear much fruit in the long run.

> **Greg:** For us, prayer with the baby started long before birth. Every night, in addition to talking with our baby in Lisa's womb, I said a little prayer of blessing over the baby that went something like this:
>
>> Lord, thank you for our wonderful baby. Please keep our baby healthy and happy and let our child know how much we love him or her already. Help us be

the mommy and daddy our baby needs, and help us to get our hearts and home ready so that we will be a perfect fit for each other.

The prayer wasn't the same every night. If the baby had a particularly active day with lots of kicking, I would pray for the baby's peace and happiness, or if Lisa felt sick that day I would pray for comfort for both of them, and so on. Of course, I'd also ask God specifically to help me be the father both the baby and Lisa needed me to be. And then I would make the Sign of the Cross on Lisa's tummy.

After the baby was born, we kept up our prayer rituals. At least once a day and sometimes more, Lisa and I would sit with the baby on one of our laps and we'd lay hands on him or her and say something like this:

> Lord Jesus, thank you for our little baby. Please fill her heart with your love, and let her know how much we love her, and give her the ability to love you and us with all her heart. Make her happy and healthy, and help her to discover all the gifts and talents you have given her so that she can lead a wonderful life and glorify you in everything she does.

Again, the prayer varied day by day, but whatever we prayed, we would end it with both of us tracing the Sign of the Cross on our baby's forehead.

Lisa: We all got a lot out of those little prayer times. In addition to those times, Greg and I would both take time to praise God when we were playing with our baby. We would kiss our baby's feet and say in a playful voice, "Thank you, Jesus, for our baby's feet! Ah, don't you have beautiful feet, little one! And thank you, Jesus, for our baby's hands! Yes, look at your hands, little one! And thank you, Jesus, for our baby's kissable face! And kissable tummy!" And we'd cover our baby with kisses. Approaching prayer this way makes conversation with God as natural as conversation with each other. And it helps introduce the baby to God in ways that are fun and heartfelt and really open up those initial avenues of grace.

Preparing for Baptism

Let's take a look at perhaps the most defining moment in your child's spiritual walk: Baptism. Here's what *The Catechism of the Catholic Church* has to say about this foundational sacrament:

> **1213** Holy Baptism is the basis of the whole Christian life, the gateway to life in the Spirit (*vitae spiritualis ianua*), and the door which gives access to the other sacraments. Through Baptism we are freed from sin and reborn as sons of God; we become members of Christ, are incorporated into the Church and made sharers in her mission: "Baptism is the sacrament of regeneration through water in the word."

> **1250** Born with a fallen human nature and tainted by original sin, children also have need of the new birth in Baptism to be freed from the power of darkness and brought into the realm of the freedom of the children of God, to which all men are called. The sheer gratuitousness of the grace of salvation is particularly manifest in infant Baptism. The Church and the parents would deny a child the priceless grace of becoming a child of God were they not to confer Baptism shortly after birth.

> **1251** Christian parents will recognize that this practice also accords with their role as nurturers of the life that God has entrusted to them.
>
> **1252** The practice of infant Baptism is an immemorial tradition of the Church. There is explicit testimony to this practice from the second century on, and it is quite possible that, from the beginning of the apostolic preaching, when whole "households" received baptism, infants may also have been baptized.[8]

Of course, the catechism has much more to say about Baptism. We encourage you to read it to have a better sense of the significance of Baptism in your baby's life. Nevertheless, we would like to offer some brief comments on what Baptism means to you and your baby.

What Does Baptism Do?

This can be tricky to talk about, but the truth is that every human person comes into the world with a sickness that has potentially serious consequences. Each and every one of us needs to be saved from this sickness—from the oldest and wisest to the youngest and smallest. What is that sickness? We call it *original sin*. Original sin is the disease that cut the human race off from complete union with God, a union that allowed us to be everything we were created to be, to know our innate dignity as God's children, and to live forever with God. Each of these graces "came standard," if you will, before the Fall. They were preloaded into the human person before original sin. Afterward, these things were lost to us until Jesus Christ conquered the evil that separated heaven and earth and enabled us to live with him eternally as part of God's family. The sacrament of Baptism continues this saving work of Jesus Christ, healing all of humankind from the continuing ravages of original sin, empowering us to reclaim our rightful place in

God's family, and enabling us to begin the journey that ends
with us living happily with him forever in heaven. Baptism
makes us a "new creation" and "sharers in the divine nature"
(2 Pt 1:4) and permanently changes us, on a fundamental level,
making us into God's own people. As Jesus himself says in
John 3:5, "Amen, amen, I say to you, no one can enter the Kingdom of God without being born of water and Spirit."

When you look at your baby through your earthly eyes, it
can be difficult to believe that there could be anything wrong
with him or her. But the truth is, just like every unbaptized
human being, your baby has a serious sickness caused by original sin. It isn't your or your baby's fault any more than any
other sickness would be, but it is real just the same. Original sin
is the sin of Adam, that spiritual sickness that robs us of union
with God and our ability to be "perfect, just as [our] heavenly
Father is perfect" (Mt 5:48). Your baby is perfectly beautiful,
but he or she was meant to be so much more! Your baby was
meant to be a son or daughter of God!

What Happens in Baptism?

In Baptism, the candidate goes under the water and then rises
up again as a sign of the candidate's participation in Christ's
death and resurrection. Full submersion isn't necessary, and
it is undesirable for infant Baptism. In some parishes, infants
will be immersed partway into the water; in perhaps most parishes, water is gently poured over the infant's head. Sacraments
cause the change they signify or point to, and so the person
baptized is washed clean from original sin as well as all other
sins (although babies can't commit personal sin). The child is
claimed for God's family (and, in a sense, takes on a new family
name), as the celebrant intones, " (*Name*), I baptize you in the
Name of the Father, and of the Son, and of the Holy Spirit."
The child is then blessed with sweet-smelling chrism oil as a
sign of the life of the Holy Spirit within the child and clothed

in a white garment symbolizing the child's purity and that he or she has become a "sharer in the divine nature."

As we saw earlier, Jesus himself states that Baptism is necessary for salvation (Jn 3:5). That is why it is important for you to seek Baptism for your child as soon after birth as you are able. Just as you name your child as soon after birth as possible to give him or her an identity, you want to make sure that your child becomes a named member of God's family and receives his or her spiritual identity as soon as possible. Parents who fail to give their children a spiritual identity from the earliest days, preferring to wait until the child can "choose what he wants to be," do their child a serious disservice. Parenting in this manner is the spiritual equivalent of not giving your child your last name just in case she may want to be part of some other family when she grows up. Perhaps your child will. What of it? Until such a sad day (and preferably, to avoid such a sad day), don't we have an obligation to teach the child what it means to be part of a family and to be a welcome and loved member of the family in which he or she is being raised?

Just as parenting doesn't end when you name your child, helping your child appreciate the spiritual gift he or she has been given doesn't end at Baptism. Again, here is what the catechism says on the subject:

> **1253** Baptism is the sacrament of faith. But faith needs the community of believers. It is only within the faith of the Church that each of the faithful can believe. The faith required for Baptism is not a perfect and mature faith, but a beginning that is called to develop. The catechumen or the godparent is asked: "What do you ask of God's Church?" The response is: "Faith!"

> **1254** For all the baptized, children or adults, faith must grow *after* Baptism. For this reason the Church celebrates each year at the Easter

> Vigil the renewal of baptismal promises. Preparation for Baptism leads only to the threshold of new life. Baptism is the source of that new life in Christ from which the entire Christian life springs forth.
>
> **1255** For the grace of Baptism to unfold, the parents' help is important. So too is the role of the *godfather* and *godmother*, who must be firm believers, able and ready to help the newly baptized—child or adult—on the road of Christian life. Their task is a truly ecclesial function (*officium*). The whole ecclesial community bears some responsibility for the development and safeguarding of the grace given at Baptism.[9]

In other words, your responsibility is just beginning. With Baptism, your child has been given an incredible gift—adoption as God's own child (*divine filiation*)! You will need to spend your life teaching your child how to appreciate this awesome gift so that he or she never forgets this deepest identity. As a son or daughter of God, your child's first and most important mission in life is to proclaim in all words and actions that Jesus Christ is Lord. As a baptized person, your child is destined for an eternal life of happiness with God and the Communion of Saints.

Eternal life is the purpose of Baptism and is at the heart of Christian parenthood. As it says in Sirach 16:1–3,

> Do not yearn for worthless children, or rejoice in wicked offspring. Even if they be many, do not rejoice in them if they do not have fear of the LORD. Do not count on long life for them, or have any hope for their future. For one can be better than a thousand; rather die childless than have impious children!

That might seem extreme, but what is the point of having children who do not live forever? Having given them life, what could be more important than giving them eternal life in heaven? Baptism is not just a social custom, a family photo op, or a nice chance to get together with the relatives. These things are the *least* of what Baptism is. Baptism is the real beginning of your child's life in Christ and the start of your formal promise to spend the rest of your life teaching your child how to live as a son or daughter of God.

> **Greg:** Each of our children's Baptisms was truly a powerful experience for me. Each time, I had a powerful sense of something very real and very amazing happening. Of course I was moved by the cuteness of our babies and the sweetness of the moment, but I also had a very real sense of heaven rejoicing at the birth of a new child of God. It's hard to explain, but I knew, not just in my head but in my gut, that God was doing mighty things in our life and in the lives of each child at his or her Baptism. I remember praying that God would give me everything St. Joseph had and more, so that I could raise our children to be God's children.

> **Lisa:** It's hard to put into words what our children's Baptisms meant to me. It was as though I could feel the Blessed Mother standing next to me with one hand on my shoulder and one hand on our children as she introduced them to our Lord. I just knew that God had great plans for each of our children, and I prayed that I could love each of them well enough so that they would feel, in the deepest part of their hearts, how much he loves them. There isn't anything I want more. I'm so glad God gave us Baptism so that my love for our children can be taken to a whole new level. My love for them is just the smallest

taste of the incredible love God has for them in his own heart. I felt that profoundly at each Baptism. God loved them even more than I did, and I loved them more than life.

The other part of the Baptism that means a great deal for me is the Final Blessing. During that prayer, first the mother(s), then the father(s), and then the entire assembly are reminded of their roles in relation to the child or children just baptized, and then all are blessed. At those moments, I experienced the overwhelming presence of God's grace. It was as though he were right there with me, giving me everything I needed to raise up our child to be everything God created him or her to be. It was breathtaking.

Be sure to talk with your pastor about scheduling your child's Baptism as soon as possible so that your child can receive all the graces and gifts God wants to give. Some dioceses require parents to take classes to prepare them for the responsibilities associated with Baptism. Don't hesitate to dive into these important sessions so that you can be ready to help your child take full advantage of the gifts of grace he or she is being given.

Choosing Godparents

"Godparent" is not a title of honor you give to a family member. A godparent is a gift you give to your child. A godparent is supposed to be someone close to your nuclear family, someone your child will see often growing up, someone who can be a representative of the larger family of faith. Spending time with his or her godparents as he or she grows up should show your child that not only do you, his parents, take the life of faith seriously, but these *other* important people who live *outside* your home and love you all deeply, take *their* life of faith seriously too.

There are many who will tell you that the role of godparent is largely ceremonial, but that just reflects what it's become for some families, not what it is. A gold bar is only a paperweight if you use it as one, and even then, it doesn't lose its original value. The role of godparent is supposed to be a powerful one. Ideally, godparents will show your children by their example that people of faith are loving, welcoming, joyful, godly people who are good and faithful company. And godparents will pray for and support you and your child as you raise your child to become everything God has created her or him to be.

All any of us can do is our best. Your child's salvation depends on Baptism, not your choice of godparents. But we urge you to take the role seriously and not treat the title as an honorific you grant to a family member or friend you happen to like hanging out with or to whom you owe a favor. Instead, try to choose the people who best represent the faith to *you*: the people you look to for inspiration when your own faith is running dry. Those are the people you want as godparents. You want Christian heroes whom you can point out to your child, saying, "Be like them."

> **Lisa:** Our children's godparents are tremendous people. It's a little unusual for all of our children to have the same godparents, but for us there was no better choice. The people we chose are good friends who really love God with everything they are. Our kids' godparents are a husband and wife who are dear friends of ours from college. The godfather is a hospital chaplain who is a loving husband, a devoted dad, and a person whose whole professional life is devoted to bringing Christ to suffering people. The godmother is a terrific, godly woman who is wonderfully thoughtful and generous with her time and talents. She remembers everyone's

birthday or anniversary and actively looks for little
ways to celebrate just how special you are to her all
year round. They inspire Greg and me like no other
two people. We're honored to be their friends, and
we've been happy over the years to point our kids
to their example of how to live a Christian life when
maybe our example hasn't been so shining.

Are you wondering who could be the best godparents to
your child? Ask yourself, "If I were really hurting and needed
to turn to a person of faith, to whom would I turn? Whose
example would inspire me to stay close to God at my worst?"
Those are the people we recommend you choose as godparents.

Choosing a Patron Saint

Raising children to be sons and daughters of God is hard work,
but ideally you don't have to do it alone. Your child's well-
chosen godparents can be a great source of support and inspiration, but in addition to the natural supports available to you,
you also have supernatural support in the form of your child's
patron saint.

As Christians, we do not believe in death. Well, we do, of
course, but we aren't so foolish as to think that death is the
end of everything. Scripture tells us that those who are asleep
in Christ are even more alive, in a sense, than we are because
they are closer to God. "Now, he is not the God of the dead,
but of the living, for to him all are alive" (Lk 20:38).

We can and should turn to the saints for their intercession
and counsel when it comes to raising our children to be as close
to God later in life as they are today. Following a long-standing,
favorite, and laudable custom in the Church, many parents
choose a *patron saint* for their children.

In ancient times, a "patron" was responsible for you. You
worked in his house, and he saw to your debts. What you did,
you did in *his* name, and you sought to model yourself after

him and make sure that whatever you did brought honor to his house. In the same way, a patron saint looks out for you, inspires you, and prays for you. The saints are alive and active. St. Thérèse of Lisieux (a.k.a. "The Little Flower") promised, with God's grace, to spend eternity doing good on earth. If you choose a patron saint for your child, ask that saint to represent your child's concerns before God and to serve as a model of the kind of character and behavior you expect from your child. Many Catholic parents name their children after their patron saints. While the Church does not require that a saint's name be chosen at Baptism, it is a wonderful and ancient tradition.

We are often given a name because of a story behind it. So-and-so was named for her uncle who liked to do X. Or so-and-so was named for her great-grandmother who was known for thus-and-such. Psychologists who study such things tell us that, assuming there is more to a child's name than "we liked the sound of it," the backstory behind the name often serves as an anchor that can powerfully influence a child's interests and character. There is a surprising body of professional literature on the psychology of names. What we are called and what we call ourselves matter a great deal on a psychological level.[10]

> **Greg:** My patron saint is Gregory the Great. He was a brilliant scholar and a deeply prayerful man who brought incredible reforms to the Church, sent missionaries to the four corners of the globe, and became known as "the Father of Christian Worship" because of his exceptional role in revising the liturgy and music of the early medieval Church. I have a deep personal affection for Pope Gregory. I like to think he has something to do with my love of music and my passion for the faith. As a kid, I was fascinated, of course, by the fact that he was called "great." I don't think I ever formed the thought consciously as a motto or anything, but I remember that

having a patron who was called "great" made me want to try harder—to strive for more. Even as an adult, I look forward to meeting him one day. I hope he will feel that I brought honor to God in his name.

Lisa: I was born Catholic, and my dad was the more faithful of my two parents. When I was five, he passed away and any meaningful religious education stopped for me. Because of that, I never really knew anything about my patron saint—Ann, mother of the Blessed Virgin Mary—until I came back to the Church as a teenager. The woman who ran my youth group took me under her wing and started teaching me about the Blessed Mother and, at some point, told me that my middle name Ann was Mary's mom's name. St. Ann is the patron saint of unmarried women, women in childbirth, and homemakers. Due to her relationship with unmarried women, there is a popular prayer for her intercession that goes "St. Ann, St. Ann . . . find me a man!" As tongue-in-cheek as that prayer can seem, I feel that her intercession led me to find Greg, and I am so grateful for that. Honestly, I don't think it's a coincidence that I came back to the Church through my youth group leader's devotion to Mary. Looking back, I can't help but think St. Ann was pushing me along saying, "Let me introduce you to my daughter . . . you'll like her. She can take it from there."

I'm so grateful for her influence in my life. Ultimately, I have to credit her for all the best things in life: my relationship with my Blessed Mother, my relationship with Christ, my relationship with my husband. Her prayers have helped make me who I am.

Is there a saint whose name is close to that of your child's name? If not, is there is a saint whose life or reputation has touched you, who you would like to inspire your child? Let that saint be your child's patron. Learn that saint's story well and share it with your child growing up. Ask that saint for his or her prayers in your family's prayer time. Celebrate that saint's feast day with a special meal, a craft, or an activity. When you cultivate your child's relationship with a patron saint, you give your child a friend for life. In fact, you give your child a friend for eternal life! And we could all use a few more of those.

Hopefully by now you see that the first weeks and months of your child's life are not just about the development of his physical and emotional well-being. There are a great many things you can do to introduce your child to the spiritual treasures that await him or her as a son or daughter of God. Take time to celebrate the rituals and establish the habits that make Christ the center of your home. When you parent with Christ, you can't lose.

PART THREE

I've Grown Accustomed to Your Face

Six to Twelve Months

The first few months have been a whirlwind. We hope that by learning to trust God's design of the human body you are beginning to see how simple and fun parenting can be, not just in spite of the effort it takes, but even because of it. The good news is that the party is just getting started!

In the next several chapters, we look at how to build on your efforts and get the most joy out of life with your six- to twelve-month-old. The last six months have brought about a lot of changes! There are many more to come, of course, but you are most likely feeling more comfortable and at ease in your parenting role now. In particular, if you have been showering your little one with affection, responding promptly to cries, and keeping your baby close, the song lyric from the musical *My Fair Lady* that gives this introduction to part three its title are applying more and more to you and your baby. You *are* more accustomed to each other's faces and sounds and gestures, and the implicit meanings hidden within them. You have become a baby whisperer to your own child. It's time to take that relationship deeper and begin applying all the skills you and your baby have been learning in new and exciting ways.

Chapter 8 covers the developmental milestones of your child's second six months of life and offers recommendations for how to understand what God is trying to tell you about your relationship with your child by "listening" to the message of his development.

Chapter 9 covers mom care at this stage, including suggestions for Dad on how to be fully engaged with Baby in a way that supports Mom. Chapter 10 begins with some considerations about returning to work after Baby and goes on to examine work-life balance both for moms who are working outside the home and for moms who aren't. Finally, chapter 11 offers some suggestions about babysitters and thoughts on marriage care at this stage.

Ready or not, your baby is growing fast. Let's look at the next stage of this great adventure and learn how to face all the exciting things to come with grace, joy, and a deep sense of the love that comes from God's own heart.

CHAPTER EIGHT

Time to Get Moving

The six-month mark brings with it big changes in your baby's mobility and interactions as well as many other exciting developments. There are many things you can do to both help your baby achieve his or her full potential and enable your family to adjust to the changes you will be experiencing over the coming months.

Lisa: By the time our little ones were six months old, we were getting around wonderfully. They were finally starting to sleep a little better, although our first was still far from perfect in that department. I remember how excited we were to see each of our babies becoming little persons at this stage. Before six months, they might have responded when you engaged them but now, each of them was starting to get the hang of the whole "interaction" thing. It is so amazing to hear babbling giving way to first words! There is nothing like that first "mama" or "dada." And of course, kids at this age are little explorers. They can't walk yet, but goodness, they sure can get around! It's amazing how fast those little guys can crawl, scoot, or roll from one place to the next.

I was so grateful that we decided to practice extended nursing because it would remind both me and the baby that we needed to take a breather. I don't think I could have gotten any of our kids to stay still if it wasn't for that and, boy, was I grateful for those quiet moments. It's funny—Mom's body might look more or less put back together on the outside, but I remember being surprised at feeling more tired and hormonal than you might expect this far along. Those quiet times for nursing breaks were a nice respite both from the baby chasing I had to do and from the errands and housework I felt more and more compelled to keep up with. I really like the idea that God is trying to talk to parents through their baby's development. If we learn to listen to what God is saying through the language of the body, Mom and Baby can make it through the first year in pretty good shape.

As you've discovered from our frequent references to John Paul II's Theology of the Body, God's fingerprints are all over creation, especially our bodies, and by studying the design of the body, we can learn something both about our Creator and about his will for how we are to live. As popular Theology of the Body expert Christopher West likes to say, "Biology is a theology."

Developmental Milestones

If we take seriously the idea that God created each of us and our children *intentionally*, then it stands to reason that we can learn something about the way God wants us to interact with our children by discerning what responses on our part cause their brains and bodies to develop to their fullest potential. Let's look at some of the developmental milestones your six- to twelve-month-old will be working on.

Sensory-Motor Milestones

Look out, Christopher Columbus and Neil Armstrong! They've got nothing on your baby, who is quickly becoming a full-time explorer. Your baby's work of coordinating his nerves with his muscles is moving beyond the basics and continuing at new levels. At around six months, your little one will start showing early signs of crawling, and by twelve months, your baby is most likely going to town (metaphorically speaking). Beginning at around eight months or so, your baby can probably sit up by himself, and over the next few months you can expect your little one to start grabbing on to anything available to pull himself up and cruising along while holding on to the edge of the couch, for example. By your baby's first birthday, you might see your child take his or her first unassisted steps!

In the seven- to twelve-month range, your baby is becoming more coordinated. It sure seems like a lot of fun to put things in a bucket and take them out again! "Look Mom! My fingers WORK! I knew it!" This skill is particularly cool at meal times, when baby can start to use his thumb and forefinger to grab tasty finger foods.

It's also fun to watch babies at this stage start to emulate big-people behavior like talking on the phone or drinking from a cup. Your little one's growing so fast!

Language Milestones

This is the time frame wherein you should hear "mama" and "dada" for the first time as your baby's nervous system starts doing a better job of coordinating the muscles in her mouth and tongue and begins moving the furniture into the speech centers of her brain. Your baby has also discovered that pointing at things often gets results! In addition to being a full-time explorer, your little one is an avid linguist. She is watching your lips carefully so that she can master this whole "word" thing you do. Pretty soon, babbling will give way to simple phrases and requests.

Social Milestones

The downside to all the exploration is a little insecurity. As Baby ventures farther from "Base Camp Mommy," he feels a little, nagging fear that maybe Mommy won't be there when he gets back. Sometimes, Baby acts as if he's thinking, "I mean, I'm pretty sure she'll still be there, but you can never be completely sure of these things, now, can you?" Remember, even now, your baby is not completely convinced that you and he are not, literally, one body (after all, you were one body for nine whole months, and he's only been "on the outside" for six months or so now, right?). The idea that he can separate himself from your body (and then reconnect again!) is new, exciting, and a little creepy-scary.

Separation anxiety is a common experience at this stage, and it tends to manifest itself in two ways: Stranger phobia and Mommy-don't-LEAVE-me! phobia. The fear of strangers at this age comes from realizing that if I'm actually *separate* from Mommy, maybe somebody could *take me* from Mommy. And we all know that is definitely not okay.

We don't mean to imply that your baby should never be away from your side. It's just that you'll need to be sensitive to the fact that it is normal for your little one to get a little stressed out if strangers get in her face or even if people she knows well—like Dad—try to take her from Mom when Baby has decided that only Mom will do.

Developmental Milestones: What Can You Do?

Carry On

Continue what you've started. Although it looks as though your baby is quickly becoming a big boy or girl, developmentally your little one is still figuring everything out—from the way his or her body works to the way the big wide world works. Your baby's brain is still growing at an incredible rate, and sometimes you can see big changes from day to day. Things seem to change like magic when quietly and suddenly your baby does something he or she couldn't do just a day earlier.

Especially because there is still so much going on, consistency in your baby's life can be very helpful. Maintaining your style of feeding and sleeping and the other baby-care rituals you established in the first six months will help Baby feel confident in what he knows and able to dedicate more of his precious resources to learning new things. Although it can seem like your little one is growing up fast, that's all the more reason to keep up the work of maintaining your connection through extravagant affection, ongoing nursing, nighttime parenting, baby wearing, and all the other practices we recommend for newborns. Doing so isn't just good for Baby—it's good for you too. God is good. He wants to encourage you in your efforts. That's why the closer you stick to your little one, the more you'll continue to receive all the physiological, psychological, and spiritual benefits we discuss in part two.

Be Patient with Transitions

At this stage, you can continue to let your baby take the lead in transitions like spacing out nursing, sleeping apart from you, and seeing how much time away from you she can handle. It is certainly fine to test things out by stretching the time between nursing a little bit or letting Grandma watch your baby a little longer. Without being overly scrupulous or anxious about it, be aware of how your baby is responding to these changes, and make the transitions as smooth as reasonably possible for all concerned. As we mention earlier, the best "schedule" is the natural rhythm that God built into your child's body. The more you can cooperate with God's schedule, the easier parenting will be for you.

PLAYING WITH YOUR BABY

> "Put on love," and your life will be like a
> house built on rock, your journey will be
> joyful.
>
> —POPE FRANCIS

Your six- to twelve-month-old is now old enough to be hip-carried in your sling. This is a wonderful way to include him or her in your daily activities and have ongoing conversations, eye contact, and kisses. You can easily get through store aisles, stroll through museums, and go just about anywhere else with ease. Have fun sharing your joys and interests with your child, and take some time at home to relax, unwind, and play.

- *Pillow mountain*: As your little one begins to crawl and climb, it's lovely for a tired mom or dad to pile up a bunch of throw pillows (not too high); while you get to rest a bit, Baby gets to climb and try new skills with your gentle hand nearby.

- *Stacking*: Little ones of this age love to stack blocks, board books, plastic cups, anything they can hold. He'll probably need your help stacking, but he'll love knocking them all down.

- *Finger painting*: With either nontoxic finger paint (if you want to keep your little one's masterpieces) or pudding or baby food (if your sweetheart is mouthing everything in sight), let her mix and smoosh. Get into it with her, even with just one finger. Draw hearts, flowers, your child's name, or simple shapes. Name them as you go. Talk about the colors you're using. Let your creativity flow. To make cleanup easy, spread a disposable or easily washed drop cloth on the bathroom floor. When you're done, all you have to do is roll up the cloth and extend the relaxing fun with a cozy, warm bath.

- *Tissue paper and paper lunch bags*: Little ones of this age love to crunch and tear this thin, soft, colorful paper. Taking it out of and putting it back into paper bags can add another element to the entertainment. Parents can place a piece of tissue paper on Baby's palm and gently blow. Your little one will love watching it fly and float.

- *Exploring ice cubes*: Place several ice cubes in an unbreakable bowl. So that the ice won't stick to Baby's skin, run some warm water over the ice cubes and spill it out. Then let his little hands chase the cubes around the bowl. This is especially good on a hot day.

- *Ball rolling*: Roll a soft ball, big enough for Baby to slap and grab, to Baby and encourage her to pick it up or roll it back.

- *Musical hide-and-seek*: This is a fun extension of the pillow mountain above. Place a wound-up musical stuffed animal under one of several pillows you've laid on the floor. Encourage your little one to find it. Make sure to clap and cheer when he finds it.

- *"How loved is Baby?"*: This is like "How big is Baby?," where you stretch Baby's arms out and say, "Soooo big!!" Only in this game, you ask, "How loved is Baby (using your baby's name)?" and then say, "Soooo loved!!" One of the beautiful things about this is that when your child is much older and sees Jesus' arms stretched out on the Cross, she will have a happy recollection of your arms stretched out with warm affection and tender love.

*Note: all these activities *must* take place while you are with your baby. Don't leave the area, even for a minute. Be sure to keep Baby safe from choking and other hazards.

Feeding

Extended Nursing

As Lisa's comments at the beginning of the chapter illustrate, there are many benefits for Baby and Mom to your continuing to nurse at least through the first year. While only about 20 percent of moms continue nursing past six months, continued nursing provides so many benefits for your baby's brain, your relationship, and your sanity that we heartily recommend getting whatever support you need to keep going if it is at all possible.

As your baby becomes more active, nursing breaks are a great way for both Mom and Baby to take a little pit stop in the middle of all the excitement and busyness. Nursing is also a great way to convince that little explorer to take a nap when he needs to instead of letting him push himself until he melts down. This is even truer for toddlers who are becoming more and more nap-resistant. When you nurse, your body produces those "calm-down" and bonding hormones for you and your baby, which can be really helpful as you start to get back into the swing of things. Likewise, extending nursing helps burn up that remaining postpartum baby weight that so many moms worry about.

Besides the benefits to Mom, breast milk continues to benefit Baby's brain and should still be the primary form of nutrition even as your little one begins trying solid foods.[1] As a best practice, you might try to hold off on giving solid foods until after your baby has nursed. Regardless, at this point, solid foods should supplement nursing, not the other way around. In fact, some babies prefer not to take solid foods until their first birthday.

Time for Solids?

Your baby will be ready to begin solid foods when he can feed himself; that is, when he can both sit up and has outgrown the tongue-thrust reflex—the reflex that has the baby's tongue slowly push everything but the breast out of his mouth, causing food to dribble down his chin instead of going down his throat. When a baby of this age pushes solid food out of his mouth, it doesn't just mean he doesn't want it. It means his body isn't ready for it.

When introducing solids, remember to start with soft foods in small amounts. Does the baby swallow or push it out? If the baby pushes the food out, wait a few days or weeks and try again. Just relax. This isn't a race, and starting solids early doesn't prove anything. Take your time. Also, try to wait a few days before introducing any new solids so you have time to watch for any allergic reactions. Allergies do not only show themselves as rashes; sometimes they manifest behaviorally, as in more crying or a shift in personality.

Teeth!

Teeth can start coming in at anywhere between three months and one year, although four to six months is average. Many moms are intimidated by the idea of nursing a baby with teeth. The mere idea can scare some moms into weaning their baby at as early as three months. But there is no need to fear. You can teach your baby not to bite you simply by immediately removing your baby from your breast at the first sign he might bite and saying loudly (but not yelling), "No! No bite Mommy!" or something similar. Your baby will quickly learn not to bite. If the baby does manage to clamp down (which is fairly unusual) simply insert your finger into the baby's mouth, gently separate his gums, and detach, saying, "No bite Mommy!" Discuss any further concerns with your lactation consultant.

Reading Time

As we note above, your baby is beginning to take on rudimentary language. He is learning the vocal "building blocks" that will eventually become words. Talking and reading to your baby are great ways to help your baby's language development. It is true that your baby will not really understand what you are saying, but that isn't the point. Every language is made up of certain sound building blocks. Talking and reading to your baby stimulates the listening and talking parts of your baby's brain and teaches your baby what sounds are most common in your language. Interestingly, a recent study in the *Journal of Pediatrics* notes that one of the reasons breast-fed babies do so much better in school and on IQ tests than bottle-fed babies is that moms who breast-feed are more likely both to respond promptly to the child's cues (which has been shown to be correlated with higher math and reading scores) and to *read* to their child. According to the researchers, parental responsiveness and reading time beginning with babies as young as nine months of age give a baby the equivalent of two to three extra months of brain development by age four.[2] This extra attentiveness and reading time actually account for a large portion of the gains in intelligence commonly attributed to breast-feeding itself. It is simply impossible to overestimate the value of reading to your child from the earliest age.

> **Lisa:** Reading time has been an incredibly important part of our family life from infancy on up through young adulthood. I loved having my baby sit on my lap and watching her light up at the sound of my voice as I told the story and pointed to the pictures. It's been such a blessing for our relationships and for developing all our kids' attention spans. At this age, reading is all about cuddles and books with textures and bright colors that the baby can touch and feel and even nibble on! Don't worry about whether the baby is "paying attention" or not. Babies are paying attention to everything whether it seems like it or not. Right now, the important thing is having your child associate with books all the warm-fuzzy feelings he has toward you! Education begins by giving

children an emotional connection with books and information.

Greg: Lisa and I both love reading to our kids, and it's an important way for me connect with them. I love making up silly voices, and babies LOVE silly voices. The sound of my baby laughing in response to my impression of a bunny rabbit's voice or reacting to Tickles the Duck is priceless. I wouldn't trade that sound for anything in the world.

Likewise, reading while nursing (or bottle-feeding) is a terrific way to get your baby to associate that comfort with reading and language. Later on, in toddlerhood, you'll be glad you took the time to do this because it gives your child another way to take a break when he or she needs it. Even if your toddler doesn't want to nurse or has weaned, he will still have a strong connection with the comforting reading ritual you've been developing in those early months and be more likely to take quiet time in your arms when he needs a break.

Sleep

Sleep is another area in which some parents try to rush things. Sometimes, parents who managed to get their four-month-old to sleep in a crib suddenly find that, at eight months, their baby is no longer happy being alone at night. (This often happens again to parents of toddlers, whose imagination begins to emerge at around twenty months). You haven't done anything wrong. Remember, in the six- to twelve-month stage your baby is *beginning* to realize that Mommy and he are not one body. This awareness is going to be especially scary when he's tired, it's dark, and he doesn't yet have even limited, beginning capacity for emotional regulation he will later develop. Also keep in mind that your baby is getting better at communicating his or her needs.

Again, we recommend that you not rush moving baby to a separate sleeping space. In our professional and personal experience, it is just simpler and better to let Baby take his own independence when he is ready to leave either the family bed or the room. Either way, if you have gotten your child to sleep elsewhere, you are not doing any harm by bringing him back to your bed if he needs you at this age. Even though babies have a little more bodily control at this age, you'll still need to be mindful of the guidelines for safe bed sharing

What does cause problems at this age is when parents lack confidence in their approach (or are arguing amongst themselves) and keep moving the baby from a crib, then into their bed, then next to their bed, then back to the crib, and so on and so on every few weeks. Inconsistency is the kiss of death for joyful parenting, and it will keep your baby up at night. All night. Every night. Whether or not you choose to follow our recommendations about nighttime parenting, your best bet is to pick an approach and stick with it.

Whatever path you choose, don't be in a rush to prove your competence or your baby's exceptionality by rushing her through various developmental stages. And if you find that, based on your baby's feedback, you were a little hasty in making a change, there is no harm in backing up a step. Independence, by definition, must be taken. It can be encouraged, but not given or forced. Let your baby show you—through her behavior—what she is ready for. Trust the signals God is giving you through your baby and adapt your approach accordingly.

Physical and Emotional Needs Are One

As in the first six months, meeting your baby's needs is as much about attachment, bonding, and emotional security as it is about satisfying your baby's physical needs. Don't give in to the idea that your child's emotional and psychological needs are somehow less important than his physical needs. They are actually one and the same.

Babies fuss and cry only if they are somehow dysregulated. An emotionally happy, engaged, and interactive baby is a physically and neurologically healthy baby. The more sensitive you are to your baby's emotional needs, the more you are actually fine-tuning response to your child's physical needs as well because, again, they are one and the same.

Keep That Sling on 'Em

We recommend sling wearing for newborns in part two, and we continue to do so for this age. In fact, slings are so versatile they can be used comfortably to carry your child up through his third year of life. Of course, your child will not need to be in the sling to the same degree at three as he does at this stage, but for now, keeping your baby close to your body and allowing him to continue to experience the rocking sensations he enjoyed in the womb is very nurturing and calming. It's a great way to let your child get some rest from all the hard work he is doing learning to control his body and beginning to explore his world!

Trust God and Your Baby

Your continued, sensitive, thoughtful, and prompt response to your baby's needs lays important groundwork for your baby's spiritual and moral development. While your baby isn't saying prayers or even consciously aware of God, your attentiveness is laying a neurological foundation for a deep sense of rightness, safety, and inner peace that makes it easier for your child to experience God's presence in a conscious, deep, and physical way later on. Your patient, attentive care is revealing God's love for your child and will help your child develop a deeper capacity for receiving God's love. There is almost universal consensus among child development experts that the relational, moral, and spiritual well-being of a child is directly dependent upon the strength of the child's attachment to his mom and dad, and attachment is solidified through extravagant affection and consistent, prompt meeting of needs. Even at this age, there is no such thing as "spoiling" a baby by giving the child affection or attending promptly to his or her needs. Doing so will certainly make the child connected to you, attached to you, and even dependent upon you, but that is appropriate and desirable at this age. *A child cannot separate until he has first learned to whom he can be most securely connected.* The child will take her own independence when she is ready— usually in toddlerhood. Forcing a child to be "independent" any earlier is a fool's errand based more on a misguided desire to prove parental competency to oneself, one's family, and friends than on the child's actual needs.

Likewise, the six- to twelve-month-old still does not have any well-established, demonstrable psychological or neurological processes that enable him to reset her various bodily systems after a stressful event. Her parasympathetic nervous system (the "calm-down" system of the brain) is still learning to do its job by watching and "catching" calmness from her mom and dad as they hold her close and soothe her with loving words and tones. At this age, God wants to give your baby the gift of peace that will last a lifetime. Through your loving care for your child, God is wiring up the calm-down systems of your baby's brain and nervous system to enable your child to be resilient—that is, to bounce back from all the trials of life she will inevitably go through. Take your time to let this gift of peace settle in both your heart and your baby's. One of the biggest mistakes newer parents make is overestimating what their baby should be capable of and treating infants as kindergarteners, kindergarteners as preteens, and preteens as college students. Relax. Take your time. Trust your child and trust what God is doing in your child through your relationship with her.

Nine Months In, Nine Months Out

The most important thing to take away from this chapter is that you should do your best to keep your baby as close as possible—day and night—for the first year. Remember, the womb experience should last nine months in and nine months out.[3] Your baby doesn't begin learning once he or she is born. She has been learning and growing the entire time she was inside of you! Her body remembers what it was like to be inside your womb, and being outside of you is strange and more than a little disconcerting! Just think of how long it takes to open your eyes in the morning after a long, dark night. How would you prefer to wake up? By letting the light in slowly and gently or by having someone throw open all the shades, turn on all the lights, and turn the radio on full blast? Which puts you in a better mood? Which enables you to listen to others and learn better? And just remember, as an adult, you have a well-developed parasympathetic nervous system that helps you rebound from the stress of waking up to a noisy world!

Now imagine what it has been like for your baby. For nine months, he was in the warm, quiet darkness of your womb. He was constantly being rocked and was gently swaddled in your womb. Suddenly, one day, all that was taken from him. He was given a whole new set of stimuli to deal with—both wonderful and strange all at once. Just like you getting up in the morning (only more so because of your child's still-developing brain), little ones do best with easy, gentle transitions. The more effort you make to give your baby at least the first nine months to adjust to this new, bright, noisy world, the happier your baby will be, the more peaceful parenting will be, and the more easily your baby will be able to take in and process all the information she needs to adapt to the exciting life to which you are introducing her.

The first year is all about taking your time, trusting what God is saying to you through your child's body, and allowing

God's work to unfold as you lovingly attend to the wonder of it all through your gentle, responsive care.

CHAPTER NINE

Attack of the Shoulds

Mom Care

At this time of Baby's life, moms get a lot of mixed messages about what they "should" be doing. By now, most moms feel that they *should* be totally back to their prebaby body, *should* have the house perfectly in order, *should* be in a regular routine of frequent date nights, and—if they haven't yet done so—*should* be returning to work (more on that in a bit).

We just want to encourage you to tune all that out. As some psychologists cheekily put it, "Please stop 'shoulding' on yourself." There is no more important work—and no more effective way to take care of yourself—than to ignore all the chatter and take regular time to enjoy and play with your baby as much as you can.

Just Play, Mom!

We know, there is so much to do and it feels lazy and selfish to "just play" with and enjoy your child—especially "so late" in the parenting game. (Goodness! Six months old! Isn't it time for him to start digging coal?!?) We also understand that the home needs to be at least basically in order and that life has to be attended to. Of course, you must do what you can here.

You need to know, however, that there is no such thing as "just play" at this stage. For your baby, play is neuroscience. It is language therapy. It is occupational therapy. It is physical therapy. It is *spiritual direction*! Everything your baby learns to do—from controlling his arms and legs, to speaking, to going from crawling to cruising to walking—is learned through play. You couldn't afford to hire all the experts you would need to duplicate all the benefits you give your baby by playing with him or her. In an address to the Pontifical Council for the Family, Pope Francis said, "When I hear the confession of a young married man or woman, and they refer to their son or daughter, . . . I always ask, 'And tell me, do you play with your children? Do you waste time with your children?' The free gift of a parent's time is so important."[1]

There you go. You have written permission from the pope. So ease up on yourself. Yes, the house should be basically safe and orderly, and Mom and Dad will have to talk (and be flexible) about the best way to get that done. Sure, dinners need to be cooked, and bills need to be paid, and errands need to be run. We are not suggesting that you should let everything go and just stare at your baby (although there are worse fates, we admit). Even so, try to work all those other, less important activities around getting ample time to just be and interact with your little one. Your baby is learning so much. She needs you to make time and show her the ropes.

Everything Else Gets Done (Thanks, Dad)

> **Lisa:** I loved playing with our babies, but I didn't come from a family that really "got" kids. Play was not a high priority in my family. So, although I loved sitting on the floor and just watching and playing with my babies, I found that I had to fight against a constant barrage of negative thoughts, things like, "You're not doing enough. You're being self-indulgent. You're taking advantage of Greg and all his hard work." I

knew how important being present to children is, I knew where I needed to be, and I genuinely wanted to be there, but those voices in my head were merciless at times.

It helped that Greg was so encouraging. Sometimes he would have rough days at work and those would be hardest because that's when I'd feel guiltiest, but we'd talk through it and he'd remind me that we were both working hard to take care of our family, each in our own way. It really helped me to be able to talk through things and have his support. Everything else—the house, the meals, bills, etc.— all that got taken care of by one or the other of us. By respecting one another's contributions, we came through in great shape.

Greg: The way I look at it is that there are certain things I can't do that Lisa can and certain things she can't do that I can. I can't lactate—much as Lisa might have liked me to at three in the morning! And though I was as engaged as I could be when I was home, I couldn't be home all day with the baby. In the same way, Lisa couldn't do a lot of the kind of work I do. But we *can* both cook and clean and do what needs to be done to take care of our household. Sometimes we can do it together, and sometimes we do what we can individually. It challenges us both to be a little more generous, but that's not a bad thing. I'm not saying it was always easy. After a ten-hour day at the office, the last thing I might want to do is come home and cook or dust, but that's not the point. Lisa was working hard at making sure our babies got everything they needed, and I was working hard . . . working. Everything else just had to get divided up however it could. We built this life together and even though it has been tiring at times, it's been and continues to be a blessing to be able to live it. I don't see it as Lisa asking me to help her. The life we've built together makes certain demands of us, and we have an obligation to see that those demands are met. She does what she can, I do what I can, and eventually it all gets done.

At this stage, and really at every stage of your child's development, Dad continues to be the most important part of the healthy mom-care plan. God is giving a great gift to both Mom and Dad by challenging them throughout the first year of their life with Baby to open their hearts in ways they never thought of. For Mom, that means letting God show her the wonder of how he created her body to attend and respond to the needs of her child. For Dad, it means discovering all the ways that he can provide emotionally and physically both for his wife and for their little one. An engaged husband and father is worth more to a healthy mom and baby than almost anything else you could imagine.

Dad and Baby

Greg: The day our oldest was born, when people came to the hospital, they expected me to be an idiot. Lisa and I still chuckle about it. I'll never get over how many of our friends and even family would comment about how surprised they were to see me carrying the baby or changing the baby. "Wow, you're really comfortable with the baby!" Meanwhile, I'm thinking, "And your point is . . . ?" Even before I became a parenting "expert," I always thought it's important for a dad to be as involved as Baby will let him be.

As the months went by, I would try to do as many baby-care activities with my wife as possible so that our babies would get used to us doing them together. Within a few days or a week or so of this, I would step in and handle things like baths or trying to comfort our child, or I would interact in different ways. Sometimes Lisa even struggled to let me in at first, and although I admit that irritated me, I didn't let myself use it as an excuse to "check out." I know a lot of guys who complain their wives "don't let" them be involved with their kids, and I get that some moms have a hard time letting go, but to me that complaint always sounds suspiciously like "I didn't really want to have to do that fathering stuff in the first place, and since my wife didn't roll out the red carpet, I get to go play video games and blame her for it."

At any rate, I didn't really need Lisa to show me what to do, but I did need our babies to see that even though my wife and I feel different and sound different and smell different, their care was similar when they were with either of us.

Of course, I developed my own rituals with our children. I had bath times covered and I did a lot of the changing (when I was home from work, anyway). I had my own way of playing with our babies, my own songs that I would sing, and my own ways of comforting them. One time, I told Lisa I was going to "hypnotize" our oldest. He was about seven months and I could tell he was very tired. First, I propped him into a sitting position on the couch. Then, I held up my index finger and moved it from left to right and back again slowly enough for him to follow it. "You are getting verrrry sleepy. Verrrrry sleepy." He followed my finger perfectly with his eyes, and each time I brought it a little closer to his face. Finally, when my finger was almost touching his face I stopped it right in front of his nose.

Hysterically, he closed his eyes and fell over on his side, sound asleep.

I was never able to get him to do it again—God knows I tried—but I got major points that night and we still laugh about it today.

Hopefully, Dad has been developing his relationship with Baby from day one. The fact that babies have a preference for the sounds and smells of Mommy doesn't mean that your baby doesn't want and benefit from ample daddy time even from the very first days after he or she is born. Babies respond to Dad's lower voice by twenty-two weeks in the womb! Daddy has different sounds, his face is scratchier and ticklier than Mommy's, and he overall feels and smells different from Mommy, but that's a good and fun thing. By now, Dad should have well-established play rituals with baby, be actively engaging in games like peek-a-boo, and be getting lots of cuddle time with Baby.

While dads can be very competent caregivers even from the very first day, especially in the early weeks it is a good idea for Mom and Dad to do as many of the baby-care rituals together as is reasonably possible so that they can learn from each other and be more consistent for Baby. Babies tolerate differences better if they emerge out of similarity.

> **Greg:** One of the things that really surprised me about that time is how close I felt to Lisa when we were caring for our babies together. We might sing a song together or pray together or just play with our kids in the tub or on the floor, but I just felt so close to her. Our church has a big statue of St. Joseph sitting with Mary in his lap and the baby Jesus sitting in her lap. I remember really connecting with that. Sometimes, when I was sitting there, holding Lisa in my arms while she was nursing the baby, I'd find myself asking St. Joseph to help me be the father

> my children needed me to be just as he was for our
> Lord.

Even though in those first weeks we recommend Dad be especially attentive to taking care of Mom, being present to Baby is a big part of mom care. The more she can see you welcoming, loving, caring for, and playing with your child, the more she can feel confident that she has someone to cover for her on those days when she doesn't have anything left to give and truly needs that break. Every mom is a little nervous about leaving baby alone with anyone else—even Dad—but the more Dad can come up alongside her and show her how he interacts with Baby and how Baby responds to him, the more peaceful she can feel about taking the breaks she needs to keep her sanity and peace.

In the six- to twelve-month stage, mom care is all about figuring out how long Mom and Baby can be apart without stressing one or the other out too much. The secret is to trust your gut. Assuming you have been attending to your child all along, you know better than anyone else what your baby can and cannot tolerate. Don't let other people talk you out of your instincts or tell you that you are just being overprotective or fussy. Parents cannot give too much time and attention and protection to a child who is still incapable of protecting him- or herself. God gave you your instincts to guide you. Trust them. The more you listen to your heart, the more skilled you will become at both mom care and baby care.

And to the dads out there, be patient with your wives. Don't push her. If you feel she is too involved, don't try to criticize her out of it, come up alongside her. The more she feels your presence, the more she sees through your behavior and your responses to the baby that you really understand what your child needs, the more she will trust you when you tell her that it's okay to step away from the baby for a date or some time alone. Don't fight her instincts. Even if she gives in, she'll just feel resentful and torn. Respect her instincts, and when she knows you really "get" her and the baby because she has seen you stepping in 110 percent, she'll come to trust your instincts, too.

CHAPTER TEN

Work-Life Balance

While the majority of this chapter is for families with moms who are either considering going back to work or are working outside the home already, every family member struggles to balance their life outside the home with their at-home responsibilities. That's why we strongly recommend that everyone at least look over this chapter for some important suggestions on how to keep giving your growing family the time it needs to bear the sort of fruit our Catholic faith says it can.

As for the question of working outside the home, although maternity leave usually ends at about twelve weeks postpartum, we are covering this issue in the six- to twelve-month section partly because there is just so much to say about the first six months that including this information in part two seemed unwieldy. But we have also decided to include it here as a way of communicating the hope that Mom will stay home as long as possible with your child. The question of whether and when to return to work outside your home is a big one, and we appreciate that faithful, well-intentioned parents will come down on different sides of this issue.

According to recent figures from the Bureau of Labor Statistics, 59 percent of two-parent households in the United States have two working parents. Overall, about 70 percent of mothers work outside the home. For many moms, the question isn't whether they will go back to work, but when. Even so, there are a few things to consider when looking at a possible return to work.

Calculate Cost versus Benefit

It is virtually assumed that an average household cannot live comfortably on one income, but financial planners almost universally agree that there is not necessarily as much to be gained by a second parent's working as it might seem up front. According to an article in *Forbes* magazine, considering the higher rate at which a secondary wage earner is taxed and assuming that child-care costs easily run between $972 and $2000 per month, it is conceivable that a mom earning as much as $50,000 (well above the US median income) would contribute absolutely nothing to the household's actual bottom line.[1]

Keep in mind that *Forbes* reached this conclusion after subtracting taxes and child-care costs only. The article referenced, but did not specifically include in the calculation, additional expenses for a secondary wage earner like a business clothing budget, mileage, wear and tear on automobiles, drinks and meals out, and other job-related expenditures. It is not unusual for a family with a second wage earner to keep less than 10 percent of the second income after taxes and expenses. But don't take our word for it. If you are considering a return to the workforce, we encourage you to search online for a second income calculator or dual income calculator and do the math for yourself. See if you couldn't make a greater financial contribution by staying home and applying yourself to such healthy money-saving strategies as buying fewer processed food products, shopping online (saves fuel costs and allows for better bargain hunting), shopping secondhand stores or frequenting yard sales (for children's clothing and toys especially), clipping coupons, and lowering utility expenses by moderating usage habits.

Our point is not to make moms who work outside the home feel bad about the financial contribution they can make. We only mean that parents should check the financial facts before they assume that there is financial pressure for Mom to leave her children to rejoin the workforce, especially if she would prefer to be home full time. There are many ways to raise a basically decent, grow-up-and-function-in-society kid, and a two-career family can certainly get the job done. That said, no one will ever take as good care of your child as you. While most studies show that children who go to day care function just fine—and do even a little better than children with *less attentive* stay-at-home moms on various measures of academic and behavioral success—this same body of research is quite clear that children who are raised by an *attentive and affectionate* stay-at-home mother do better on all measures of success than children raised in any other environment.[2]

Moms who would like to return to work in order to protect professional careers they have worked hard to establish should also do a cost-benefit analysis. This is a delicate balancing act that requires prayerful discernment and consideration of the question, "How can Mom meet her needs while still giving Baby the best possible care?" For the time being, ask yourself what would be necessary to keep up licensures or certifications while remaining home as much as possible. Working from home on a limited basis or taking on consulting positions that give you the greatest possible degree of flexibility are ways of protecting your investment in your professional life while still being present to your child.

Be Creative and Flexible

We recommend doing as much as you can to truly enjoy this season of your life as parents *first*. There is nothing wrong with wanting to return to a career or wanting to keep up credentials you worked hard to earn, but be careful not to let these things become your identity. If we gave up our radio program, counseling practice, and writing today, there would be another show on the air, another therapist seeing our clients, and another book taking the place of this one in bookstores tomorrow. The world would not miss a beat. The only jobs in which we can never be replaced are spouse and parent. Knowing this from the beginning of our marriage, we have worked hard over the years to make sure our work always allowed us both to put our marriage and family life first. We work from home. We homeschool. We have always turned down speaking engagements and other opportunities—some quite glamorous—that don't allow us to travel with our children. And if you think it's easy for us because we have achieved a certain level of success and notoriety that makes such choices more accessible to us than the average bear, don't kid yourself. When we had our first baby, Greg quit his good job to open a private practice starting with only five clients a week—and this was long before we even thought of writing a book or appearing on radio or television. Lisa is a teacher by training and loves the classroom. She chose to homeschool and tutor and care for other people's children after school rather than return to the workplace in our early years as parents.

> **Lisa:** My experience growing up really drove home to me the importance of putting family first. My dad was one of the founding producers of CBS's iconic *60 Minutes* news program. He won two Emmys and a Peabody for his work with great newsmen Mike Wallace, Harry Reasoner, and Morley Safer. He got to live for a time at the Kennedy compound. He was smuggled into Cuba to interview Castro in a cave before the revolution and counted royalty, heads of state, and celebrities as friends. My dad travelled the world, and by all accounts he had an amazing life. He was also a great and loving dad—when he could be home. I have great memories of sitting on a raft clamming with him when I was two or three,

squealing and trying to keep the mud and shells from touching my feet while he laughed and we splashed each other. But obviously he had to travel a lot for work, and he was often away for weeks at a time. He always told my mom that it was okay for him to be away so much when my sister and I were little because we didn't need him so much then. He said we'd really need him when we were teenagers, and by then he'd be established and things would settle down. Sadly, my dad never lived to see our teen years. He developed a brain tumor and died when I was only five and my sister was twelve. I still have one of his Emmys. (My sister has the other). The gold gilding is flaking off. The inscription is worn. Nobody remembers him at CBS anymore, but I think of him every day. And I would give anything to have time with him again.

We know from our professional studies as well as our personal experience that making choices and even taking risks to put family first is worth it. It absolutely hasn't always been easy, but through it all, we have been blessed with an uncommonly intimate, joyful, and rewarding marriage and family life that make the sacrifices well worth our efforts. We understand that the choices we have made are not for everyone, nor are they possible for everyone. That isn't our point. The point is that as Catholics, we are called to give radical witness to the value of marriage and family life. Each of us must do this in our own ways, but we must do it. The best way to take up this challenge is to pray each morning, "Lord, give me the courage to make the choices that allow me to put my family first." This is a great prayer for stay-at-home moms and dads as well as moms and dads who work outside the home. It has made a tremendous difference in our family life and we're sure that it will in yours as well, no matter what its size and shape.

Many Ways to Be a Catholic Family

There are many ways to be a great Catholic family. Some great Catholic families have a stay-at-home mom or dad, some have both parents working outside the home, and still others, through circumstance, have a single parent. But the one thing all great Catholic families have in common is that they realize that any work they do has to be at the service of their family life and what's genuinely best for their marriage and their children. Pray with your spouse about the best way to achieve this balance in your life. Start and end each day with a firm intention to put your family first, and trust the Lord to guide you toward achieving the balance he is calling your family to exemplify.

If You Return to Work

The Catechism of the Catholic Church speaks of the importance of meaningful work to the dignity of the human person but reminds us that, to be healthy, work must exist to serve the good of the person and the family. Any work that undermines the dignity of the person or the integrity of the family constitutes an injustice that we must try, in whatever simple ways we can, to overcome.[3]

All of this means that while sometimes we need to work outside the home and sometimes we want to work outside the home, it is important for both our well-being and that of our little ones that we be as fully present to our family as we are able, even if that causes us to live in some degree of tension with our circumstances. Whether parents work in the home, work from home, or work outside the home, all of our work must be in service to the family—not just the financial needs of the family, but the emotional and psychological and spiritual needs, too. Maintaining our bond with our children regardless of our work status has to be job number one. If you do decide to return to work, there are things you can do to maximize your ability to continue to bond with your child and minimize your stress.

Work from Home

First, consider opportunities that allow you to work from home. Telecommuting options are increasing in almost all professions and, in these instances, can be a great way to meet everyone's needs. Many of our readers know that Lisa and I host a daily radio program and that we are the coauthors of several books. Fortunately, we are able to do all this from our home and at times that do not interfere with our ability to be present to our children. Lisa regularly steps away from the microphone if one of the children needs her during the show. In fact, when our youngest child, whom we adopted from China, was an infant, she would rest in a baby sling on Lisa's lap while we were on the air. She enjoyed being on Lisa's lap for the show so much that as a toddler she began wearing a pair of little black earmuffs so she could pretend to have her own headset! She would chat with our engineer during breaks, and she knew to be quiet and color when she heard the music. If she ever began to fuss, Lisa would simply step away for as long was necessary to comfort her and then rejoin me on the broadcast. We also do most of our writing in the evening after the kids are in bed. In this way, we're both able to share in the childcare and much of the ministry work we do. We find the experience to be very rewarding for our marriage and, since we have been able to work in a way that doesn't absent us from our kids, it works for our family too.

If working from home isn't a realistic option, here are some suggestions for maintaining your connection with your child and staying sane.

Try Working in Shifts

Many parents work in shifts to enable at least one parent to be with Baby at all times. Although it takes more effort to maintain your marriage with this option, there is no question that no one will take care of your child as well as you—assuming you are an attentive and affectionate parent.

Mark is restaurant manager and Anna Grace is a dance teacher. Their respective jobs required them both to work a lot of nights and weekends. When they had their first child, they wanted to make sure that their little girl would have at least one of them present at all times. Since Mark had more employment opportunities available to him, he quit his job and took another position that would not require him to work evenings and weekends. It was a bit of a sacrifice, because he was actually up for a promotion, but Mark felt it was worth it. Since he made the change, Anna Grace stays with the baby during the day and he takes evenings and weekends. They're creative about getting time together. Occasionally, he can come home for lunch instead of staying at the restaurant, and sometimes she is able to let her assistant run a class so they can get a date. Together, they work it out, knowing this will not last forever and that their marriage can sustain the sacrifices.

Family Member Child Care

The next obvious family-friendly idea is having a family member provide care. Less obvious is to try to make sure that the baby is familiar with the caregiver before you drop him or her off. People often think that babies don't care who takes care of them as long as their needs are basically handled. This is not the case. Babies are extraordinarily aware of their environment, and even though they don't always have very specific ways to communicate their preferences, they certainly have them. Invest time in your child's transition to childcare with a family member by making sure that family member gets ample time with you and your little one together before you have to leave him or her with the caregiver and return to work. Let your baby understand that this new person and you "go together" so that the transition will be smoother and make more sense to your child.

Community Day Care

Often there are no other options except making use of a community day-care program. A good day-care program has a minimum of one staff member for every four babies they are caring for. We recommend that you find an even lower baby-to-staff ratio if possible. (If you wonder why, imagine yourself at home with four babies under a year old and you'll start to get a sense of the answer. How likely is it that one person will really have the energy to fully attend to four babies?) Before returning to work, make sure to spend as much time as possible in the day-care center helping your baby get accustomed to the new environment and new people. Also, let the day-care program know that you will be dropping in as you are able—certainly in the first few weeks—just to make sure your baby is adjusting well. If the day-care provider objects to your presence for any reason—even good-sounding reasons—choose another day-care provider.

Integrating Outside Care into Your Family's Life

Use Transitional Objects

If you must be away from your child for longer periods because of work, make sure to give the care provider (family or community) plenty of transitional objects. Give them something that smells like you. To accomplish this, sleep with the small stuffed animal you will be leaving with your child, or tuck a small baby blanket inside your pajama top when you go to sleep. You might also leave one of the many brands of soft cloth books that allow you to insert family pictures into them. Similarly, have a special toy that contains a recorded message like "I love you and I'll see you soon." Or, you might even have a few books that allow you to record your voice reading the story. While these are not perfect solutions, all these objects can help your baby stay connected to you while you are away.

Spend Time with Baby during Transitions

Resist the temptation to see drop-off and pickup as just one more chore. Well-attached babies often cry for a bit when they know they are going to be left. They may also tend to act a little standoffish at first when you pick them back up again. This is normal and appropriate. A baby who is too easily dropped off and picked up and makes no protest either way is not as securely attached as a baby who fusses at least for the first few minutes.

Although it may seem counterintuitive and even be against what the day-care workers recommend, stick around until your baby settles down. Say your goodbyes, give your baby to the child-care provider, and then just hang out for a few minutes. When your baby seems engaged in his new environment, take your leave.

Likewise, when you return, if he seems a little standoffish, take a few extra minutes to sit by your child and greet him in a gentle voice. Let him get used to you again. As soon as he'll let you, pick him up and hold him close. Better still, put him in his sling. Sling wearing is a great ritual that fosters security and lets baby know that Mommy is "all mine" again!

Finally, make a point of learning the songs and activities that go on at your child's day care. Sing those songs and play those games at home. The more you can do to create continuity between home and day care and vice versa, the better.

Solidify Routines and Rituals

While routines and rituals are important for every baby, babies in daycare experience extra stimulation that can make life a little more confusing. To aid his sense of security, it can be important to give the child a clear sense of what to expect when he is with you. What can the child count on? Be organized and intentional about bath time, bedtime, and mealtime routines. These are not merely activities to complete—they are rituals of bonding and connection. Remember Mother Teresa's famous comment that the path to holiness lies in doing "small things with great love." Try to apply this to all the little rituals you share with Baby. Also, be clear about who does what at this age. Give your baby a clear sense that Mommy always does *this* with me, Daddy always does *that*, and Mommy *and* Daddy always do *these things*.

The more your baby can count on life to be a certain way with you, the easier it will be for him to decompress after a long day at the office!

Make the Most of Nighttime Parenting

Though we recommend it for every parent, we recommend bed sharing even more highly for families with a working mother. You wouldn't think that your presence at night would make that much of a difference, but it does! Your baby's brain is wired to automatically synch up with your breath and body sounds, to recognize your smell, to know your sounds. The closer you can be at night, the better.

> Beverly went back to work when Emily was twelve weeks old. "My maternity leave was up, and I had to go back to work. I really felt conflicted about it, but my husband's job is not very secure and we felt that his situation really required me to work. Although it's hard most days to be away from Emily, I just love cuddling her at night. It's great to be able to wake up even for a few seconds at night and see her curled up next to me. She loves to dig her feet under my side! It's not the most comfortable thing, but I've come to really appreciate that she wants to be that close to me. I'd like to be home full time, but until then, we get a lot of special moments together at night—even when she's sleeping.

Make Weekends about Family

We are all busy, and this is especially true of the two-career family. Work and other commitments tend to squeeze out the most important activity we can engage in: family life itself. Too many families are merely collections of individuals living under the same roof. Catholics are called to always think of family as a school of love where we learn all the virtues that enable us to live life as a gift.[4] As Pope Francis explained in an address to the Pontifical Council for the Family, *a family isn't simply a group of individuals, but it is a community where people learn to love one another.*[5]

When both parents work outside the home, the weekend often becomes the time to focus on almost exclusively chores and errands. Obviously things need to get done. But our strong recommendation is that you do them together as much as possible. Put your baby in the sling, and bring her along as you do the errands, do the grocery shopping, clean the house, or whatever needs to be done *together with your spouse.* Many families fall into the trap of thinking that "divide and conquer" is the quickest way to get everything done. But this approach merely divides your family and conquers your ability to have any kind of time together. By the time you're done running around by yourself or staying by yourself with the baby all day (or worse, running around while your baby is at the sitter again), you're all exhausted, you don't know each other, and you're too tired to care. Of course some degree of "divide and conquer" for chores and errands can be fine; especially if you time it so that if one of you gets ready quicker than the other (ahem, dads, we're talking to you here) the quick one can get started on a few projects or errands while the spouse is getting ready. Then, once you're both ready for the day, do what's left together.

Especially for the two-career family, weekends need to be family time. It doesn't all have to be amusement parks and fun time. As you've seen throughout the book, family time can consist of any number of activities that involve working, playing, talking, or praying together. But you have to get over the mindset that chores, errands, and tasks are things you push through so you can get family time. All this attitude will get you is less and less family time. Make chores, errands, and tasks part of family time. While you're cleaning, put on some music and dance with your baby in the sling. When you're out getting your shopping done, stop for some ice cream. Chores, errands, and tasks are *an important part of your life*, and if you do them together, you are living the life you've created with each other. And if you make a point of asking yourselves, "How can we do this task in a way that might be a little more pleasant or enjoyable?" you'll find ways to bond and take care of each other the whole time.

Make Fun a Family Affair

One last thing to keep in mind, especially if you are two-career family, is that your need to prioritize your weekends for family time will necessitate severely curtailing other personal activities, hobbies, and distractions. That may sound like a huge sacrifice, but trust us, it's worth it. The more you spend time on these other pursuits—fun and rewarding as they may have been before you became parents—the more you will pay for it with a family that doesn't know how to get along. You need to spend time together to learn to get along with each other. Quality time is a myth. It takes *quantity time* to learn how to interact with each other and to maintain the quality of those interactions. Since you don't have that time during the week, you are going to have to make sure you get it on the weekends. Trust us; even if it feels like a sacrifice at first, it won't once you commit to it. Why? Because investing your nonwork time into your family life almost exclusively will empower you to experience your family as a restful, enjoyable retreat. You will find yourself surrounded by the people you not only love the most, but have the most fun being around. If you want to maintain a hobby or participate in an extrafamilial activity, try to figure out a way to do it as a family.

> **Lisa:** When our kids were babies, we decided to join a community theater production of *A Christmas Carol*. Acting is much more Greg's thing—I'm usually much more of a behind-the-scenes kind of person. But he really wanted to try out, so we decided that we would do it if we could all be in the play. The kids and I got parts in the chorus (our oldest was four and our second was still in a baby sling—onstage!) and Greg had a dual role as Marley and Old Joe. We went to practices together and had a great time doing it. It was fun to support Greg in doing something he enjoyed and to share that experience together, and he really appreciated the sacrifice I made to do something that wasn't really my thing. Honestly, though, it wasn't much of a sacrifice. I had to leave my comfort zone, but I had so much fun that first year we did the play as a family for five years running after that. We have a lot of great family memories from that time!

Called to Reflect the Catholic Vision of Love

Are we saying that you have to do everything together all the time? Well, no. (Although we think there could be much worse fates.) But we are saying that having the kind of family life we all crave—that joyful, grace-filled family life where moms and dads and kids genuinely like being around each other—requires countercultural thinking and real effort. We can tell you from both personal and professional experience that the payoff is huge; but to become the kind of family that genuinely witnesses to the Catholic vision of love—a vision that children are a blessing and that marriage is a sign to the world of the love that comes from God's own heart—you have to think a little differently than your neighbors might about arranging your priorities and spending your time.

Spiritual masters tell us that the Christian journey is a call to intimacy. As we mature spiritually, God calls us deeper and deeper into union with himself. He won't rest until we are completely and totally one with him. Married couples learn to be one with God by first learning how to be one with each other. That takes work, and prayer, and thought. But this is the Little Way of holiness that is family life. This journey we are inviting you to take—to create a uniquely grace-filled family that truly reflects the Catholic vision of love—is going to make you think, look, and act differently than many of your friends and coworkers. Some people will even think you're crazy, chasing after some ideal of family unity and intimacy that doesn't exist. But that's why God gives the world Catholic families like you: to show those people that they have been sold a lie—that there *is* more love to be had for those who are willing to make the sacrifices for it and to ask God to show them how to do it. Families like yours can show the world that a family that loves, struggles, and celebrates together and connects with one another in faith and intimacy truly can exist.

We realize this might strike some of you as a radical idea. It certainly remains countercultural in many respects. The world will tell you that unless you are engaged in three thousand extra activities, hobbies, and personal pursuits, your life can't be meaningful. But whether you work out of the home or are a stay-at-home parent, remember that of all the things you do, the most life-changing, soul-satisfying, meaningful activity is learning how to suck the marrow out of life by discovering God's plan for love written on the hearts of your spouse and children. It takes time to learn to read the manuscript, but those who take the time to do it are never sorry.

CHAPTER ELEVEN

Just the Two of Us

Marriage Care

If you have been following the suggestions we made in chapters 3 and 6, you should be in pretty good shape at this point. We hope that you've been maintaining your regular rituals of work, play, talk, and prayer as a couple and that these have enabled you to stay close. Likewise, we hope you've been flexible and creative about taking your baby with you on dates and having dates in as needed. Maintaining these connecting rituals as well as taking full advantage of the fun, closeness, and partnership you and your spouse can cultivate even while Baby is around will constitute the majority of what keeps your marriage going strong. We cannot overemphasize the importance of keeping up the marriage care practices we have recommended so far in this book.

All that said, it is always a wonderful treat to get some actual, honest-to-goodness one-on-one time with your spouse, even if it is only a few hours. In the six- to twelve-month age range, it becomes reasonably possible to begin getting at least some time alone together. The trick to success is taking it slow and learning, over time, the strategies that work for both you and Baby. As before, the Three Cs of creativity, consultation, and commitment will go a long way.

Tips for Leaving Baby with a Sitter

As we note in chapter 8, although separation anxiety is common at this stage, some babies handle being left for shorter periods (perhaps two hours or so) fairly well, and some even a little longer. The key to handling these transitions is using caregivers with whom your baby is very familiar and having the caregivers come to your home. The more familiar your baby is with both sitter and surroundings, the more successful your time away from Baby will be. Everything we write about childcare in chapter 10 applies here as well. The best way to get the baby ready to be left with a sitter is to have the sitter come to your house several times and spend time with you and the baby together—and this includes grandparents and other family members, who don't get a special pass with Baby just because they are related! Baby doesn't know who she is related to. She only knows who she has spent time with. A sitter who has spent time with you and your baby together will be able to learn your baby's cues better, which will make things much easier for both your baby and your sitter.

The best way to leave your baby with a familiar sitter is to invite the sitter to begin playing some game with you and your baby. When your baby is engaged with the sitter, excuse yourself casually. Wait a few minutes to see how things go, and then leave. You don't have to sneak out, but don't make a big show of leaving. At this age, babies don't understand "hello" and "goodbye." They only know "I see you" and "I don't see you." When you return, try to do it the same way. Have the sitter engage the baby in some simple game, and start playing with the two of them. When the baby is reengaged with you, take your baby in your arms and have some extended cuddle time while the sitter packs up to go.

As we note in chapter 10, it is normal for securely attached babies to fuss a bit when they know they are going to be left (as if to say, "Please stay!") and be a little standoffish when you return (as if to play hard to get). This is normal and appropriate. Remember, contrary to popular wisdom, the baby who handles transitions from your care to someone else's too easily may not be as securely attached as the baby who makes at least a little bit of a protest. Even so, this resistance shouldn't last more than a few minutes. Assuming you handle the transitions in the sensitive way we recommend, you should do just fine.

Another idea we discussed in chapter 10 is the use of transitional objects that remind your baby of you. Keep a few special toys in reserve for your date nights. These toys could include any number of soft cloth books that allow you to insert your picture, or a stuffed bear with a recording of your voice saying, "I love you!," or even a small storybook that allows you to record yourself reading it aloud. These special treats are both novelties that can capture your baby's interest and reminders of you that can help calm your little one when he starts to miss you.

Despite all these preparations, because babies are fickle and because separation anxiety is fairly common at this stage, be sure not to go too far away, and leave your cell phone on! This way if your baby needs you, you won't be long in returning.

A little sensitivity goes a long way in meeting both your needs and your baby's. If you take your time and don't put too much pressure on yourself to make *this* date the fulfillment of all your dreams and/or the test of how strong your marriage *really* is, you and your baby will work out the best way to manage these transitions. Keep learning over time through trial and error, and you will be able to find the best ways to get the alone time you need with your spouse while giving your child everything he or she needs to remain secure in your love.

Building Your Marriage IQ

In addition to maintaining the routines and rituals in your marriage and family, taking advantage of time with baby to talk and connect with each other, and getting those occasional date nights, this is a good time to start refocusing a bit more effort on your marital relationship. A good way to do this is by picking up good books on marriage. We recommend our *For Better . . . FOREVER!*, *The Exceptional Seven Percent*, and *Holy Sex!*; as well as books by respected marriage experts like Dr. John Gottman of the Gottman Institute (*Ten Lessons to Transform Your Marriage*, *The Seven Principles for Making Marriage Work*), Dr. Scott Stanley from the University of Denver (*A Lasting Promise*, *The Power of Commitment*, *Fighting for Your Marriage*), and Dr. Sue Johnson at the University of Ottawa (*Love Sense*, *Hold Me Tight*) to name a few.

Additionally, we recommend looking for marriage days of reflection hosted by your diocese or a local parish. You might consider attending or hosting our *A Marriage Made for Heaven* marriage enrichment program in your parish. This is a series of twelve monthly meetings for couples. Each lasts for only a few hours but focuses on a specific theme (including marriage after kids), and contains a brief video teaching, discussion questions, and exercises to help you and your spouse take your marriage to a deeper level. These programs can be a great way to learn new relationship skills and meet other couples who take their faith, marriage, and family life seriously. Developing friendships that can support you through the ups and downs of the early years of your family is invaluable.

Another common way couples reconnect is through programs like Worldwide Marriage Encounter (www.wwme.com) or Retrouvaille/Rediscovery (www.helpourmarriage.com). These are great resources for couples, but because they are weekend-long experiences, unless you feel that your marriage urgently needs a focused tune-up, we would recommend holding off on any overnight marriage retreats until your child is a little bit older and is used to your being away for slightly longer periods.

The best gift parents can give their children, besides prompt response to children's cues and extravagant affection, is to love one another. Now that your little one is beginning to develop some sense of him- or herself, this is a great time to rediscover your couplehood—the core of your marital vocation—and recommit to loving each other well and deeply.

Hitting Your Stride

Twelve to Twenty-Four Months

You're probably starting to feel like a pro by now, but as with every stage of life, just as you are becoming an expert at what you've been doing, new challenges and new opportunities for joy present themselves.

In part four we look at the beginnings of toddlerhood. Parents often hear that toddlerhood can be a terrifying time. To that we say, "Be not afraid!" Toddlerhood can be one of the most magical and wonderful times of childhood if you approach it with the right spirit and the right tools.

Chapter 12 looks at the importance of maintaining your close relationship with your toddler and also at the developmental milestones your child will be reaching. Chapter 13 examines the basis of healthy toddler discipline and lays out the three Rs of toddler discipline. Chapter 14 explores mom care, which at this stage of the game can involve dealing with some maternal brain rot, loneliness, and getting caught in the crossfire of the so-called "Mommy Wars." Finally, chapter 15 looks at spiritual care of the toddler with a special eye toward taking your toddler to Mass.

CHAPTER TWELVE

Supporting Your Little Explorer

One of the continuing themes of this book is the need to trust what God is doing in your baby. The Theology of the Body asks us to prayerfully take our cues for cultivating healthy relationships from how God designed our bodies to function at their best. This approach has led us to recommend parenting practices that support your baby's brain development, such as showing extravagant affection, extended nursing, keeping baby close, baby wearing, and even nighttime parenting. The point of following these recommendations is not only to do what is best for your baby, but to do what is best for you by making your family life and parenting career as joyful and carefree as possible.

A Foundational Relationship, Not a Set of Techniques

Please remember that these recommendations are not supposed to be techniques, things you do to your baby to make him turn out right. Your baby is not a machine, and this is not an operating manual that tells you what buttons to push to get the results that will make you feel good about yourself.

Rather, all along, these recommendations have been aimed at helping you learn the language your baby speaks: the language of touch and sensation, a language whose vocabulary is cuddles and whose grammar and syntax is intensive face time. The more fluent you are in the language of "baby," the stronger your relationship will be—the more your baby will learn to synch his body rhythms to yours and the more you will learn to understand each other's facial expressions and cues. By speaking this language with your baby, you have been learning how to read the parenting manual God has written on your baby's heart.

We bring this up because many parents approach the kinds of recommendations we make throughout this book with the idea that these are all just *techniques* you *have* to use if you want your baby to be okay, and the sooner you can stop all this nonsense and fussing and get on with parenting "like everyone else" the better. To be honest, if that is your mindset, it would be better for you not to try anything in this book, but to adopt a more conventional parenting approach from the beginning because you will only confuse and frustrate both yourself and your child by sending mixed messages. What do we mean? Well, when you follow the recommendations we have been making, everything about your parenting style says to your child, "Come closer. Learn from me. Listen to my body. Look at my face. Read my lips. Calm down. Focus. Let me teach you what it means to *be*."

Unfortunately, when you follow the recommendations in this book with a "when can I finally stop doing all these techniques and get back to real life" attitude, you send a very different message with your emotions and demeanor—something like, "Hurry up, kid. You're holding me back. Haven't I done this enough already? I have stuff to do that you're keeping me from." Please understand that we all have moments when we feel this way. That's completely normal, and you shouldn't stress out or feel guilty about it. But if this is your prevailing attitude—if nine times out of ten you feel trapped or resentful or crazed by this approach, you will need to challenge yourself to get past this attitude in order to get any of the benefits of the practices we've been recommending. Let's explore why by way of an analogy.

Imagine going on a date with your spouse because you two have read in some book of the importance of employing the "technique" called "date night." You go out with your spouse, but the entire time your mate is checking his phone, frowning, calling the office, looking bored or stressed, and talking to you in clipped tones. Now imagine that you complain to your spouse and he says, "What? I did what the book said healthy couples do! We're doing the regular 'date night' technique! What's your problem?" You went on the date, but did you get anything good out of it? Of course not. Attitude is everything in a relationship. The same is true of the relationship with your baby.

Your Toddler Still Needs That Relationship

We bring this important distinction up now because the twelve- to twenty-four month stage is when your baby begins displaying the first signs of real independence. He is probably beginning to walk unassisted (or will be soon—relax!), and by about twenty-four months he fully understands that he is a separate being from you, not just an extension of your body. Because of this milestone, many parents treat this stage like a graduation from attachment. They think, "Finally! I can finally stop all these techniques the 'experts' said I *had* to use (or else!) to prevent my baby from becoming an axe murderer. Now I can just be a normal mom or dad and stop all this nursing and holding and fussing."

You may certainly do this if you wish, but if you do, you will have missed the entire point of the first year of your baby's life. Hopefully, by doing the kinds of things we have been recommending, you have been learning as much from your baby as she has from you. You have been learning how to slow down, how to be calmer about life in general, how to focus on relationship and intimacy, and how to read your baby's cues and signs and signals. You have been learning that there is a whole world beyond busyness and rushing and producing. You've been learning how to hear, on a deeper level, God's call to intimacy that rests at the heart of the Christian journey, and you have been learning how to live life to the full.

Developmental Milestones

Regardless of how you have been evolving, over the next twelve to twenty-four months (and beyond), your baby will be evolving out of the language of touch and sensation and start-ing to learn, in earnest, the language of words and symbols; but for now, your baby is just beginning to be bilingual. Up until about twenty-four months (and really even thereafter, because from about eighteen to twenty-four months of age the aver-age toddler is still only speaking one- or two-word phrases), despite the growing signs of independence and intellect, your baby's primary language is still touch and sensation, and this remains the best way to communicate with her. That's why we recommend on the pages ahead that you keep up many of the practices you have been doing all along—not because they are the techniques you need to use to make sure your child turns out okay, but so that you can continue to speak to your child in the language that makes most sense to her. By doing so, you will continue to effectively teach the lessons she can learn best through this language of touch and sensation instead of sud-denly refusing to speak to her in her first language. If you shift the way you interact now, you will simply be jabbering away at your child in a language (words and symbols) the rudiments of which she won't begin to master for at least another year.

Physical Milestones

The most significant milestones you will see in your baby's second year are related to mobility—*walking* is a huge achievement. At around ten to twelve months, your baby was pulling himself up on the edge of the couch and trying valiantly to walk the length of it. Now he is mastering two-legged movement. Your baby will probably start enjoying toys on wheels that allow him to push and pull them along with him as he explores the world with ever-greater confidence. By twenty-four months your baby may begin *running* and, yes, running away from you to make you chase him—especially when you have asked him to "come here right now." It might feel like defiance, but it really isn't. It's just so much fun to run (and it's absolutely *hysterical* to watch you do it!) that your toddler has a hard time imagining that someone wouldn't want to do it all the time.

This is also a time for *climbing*. Remember, twelve to twenty-four months is all about building those gross-motor skills. Babies at this age want a challenge, and if you don't give them one, they'll find their own by climbing on tabletops and counters, where they could get hurt. The best way to prevent this is to anticipate their need to climb and take them to objects you feel it would be okay for them to climb on. For instance, you might stack cushions to let them climb up onto the couch with your supervision or get baby stairs that allow them to climb up onto your bed with supervision. If they learn that climbing is something that they do with you and that you will facilitate, they will be less likely to do it on their own under more dangerous conditions.

Hold Hands or Hold You

Speaking of danger, most importantly, this is age where it is important to adopt the *"hold hands or hold you"* rule.

> **Lisa:** A lot of our friends complain about this age, especially the later months, because this is the time when their kids start taking off: running in parking lots, bolting out the door into the yard, and the like. I have to say we never had that problem because

of the "hold hands or hold you" rule. The idea is that unless we are in the house, one of us parents is either holding the child's hand or holding the child. And we always say, "Remember, hold hands or hold you," before opening the door or taking the child out of her car seat. Likewise, when we're walking, at the first sign that the child is trying to take off without us, we scoop her up and carry her. When the child fusses about wanting to be put back down, we repeat the rule: "Hold hands? Or hold you?" If the child continues to fuss we will put her down again and let her walk as long as she holds hands, but the moment she starts to pull on us as if she is trying to run away, the child is back in our arms. After a short while every child learns that to be allowed to use the freedom that comes with feet, she needs to stay close to a grown-up who can teach her how to use those feet safely!

We talk more about toddler discipline in chapter 13, but you might already be getting the hint that at this age, an ounce of prevention is worth a pound of tantrums and tears.

PLAYING WITH YOUR TODDLER

> I ask you to swim against the tide; yes, I am asking you to rebel against this culture . . . that ultimately believes you are incapable of . . . love. I have confidence in you and I pray for you. Have the courage . . . to be happy.
>
> —POPE FRANCIS

Your little one will grow in size and capability very quickly during the next year. Play with this toddler becomes more creative and entertaining every day. Participate, observe, and enjoy your little genius as he or she starts to puzzle things out, role-play, and discover the world in more detail every day. There are many wonderful ideas on the Internet for play at this age if you need to jog your imagination.

- This is a great age for beginning *pretend play*. Have simple costumes for your child to dress up in. You can find great ones at consignment or thrift stores such as St. Vincent de Paul, Salvation Army, or Goodwill stores. Or check out yard sales. You might find whole costumes or fun odds and ends to create your own with your toddler's "help." Toy stores also sell many costumes in toddler size.

- *Silk scarves* or three-by-three-foot squares of different-colored silk are wonderful for imaginative play. They can be fashioned into costumes, draped over chairs to make forts, wrapped around baby dolls as blankets, or twirled through the air as your child dances. I bought a set of these for one of my children and they have lasted for years and years of creative play.

- *Play food* is very fun at this age. You and your child can play store, restaurant, picnic, food show, and on and on. There are many different kinds of play food, from wooden to plastic to fabric. Many kids have a tactile preference. It can also be fun to have the kind that comes in sections and Velcros together so your child can practice cutting and chopping.

- *Sensory bins* become wonderful fun at this age. There are tons and tons of wonderful ideas for sensory play. They engage children in wonderful exploring and learning through their senses and often help to calm a child as well. Most bins can be created from a dish tub or an inexpensive storage bin. I love the ones that come with lids so that I can cover and store the bin for use at another time. One easy example is a bin filled with cornstarch and nonchokeable objects for your little one to find hidden in it. Another is to use food coloring to dye uncooked rice. Place the different colors of dried rice in different cups, and let your child pour them into the bin. Mix the rice with wooden spoons. Pour it through funnels. I found the most relaxed way of doing this was to set my child up on an old sheet. If the rice spilled over the container, I only had to lift the sheet at its edges to slide the rice to the center, making cleanup quite simple.

- *Play snow* is great fun, but requires careful parental attention to make sure your little one doesn't put it in his mouth. Mix two sixteen-ounce boxes of cornstarch and one can of shaving cream. It turns into a substance that looks and behaves a lot like snow, including being cold to the touch. Help your little one roll it into balls, and you can make your own indoor minisnowmen. It's a good idea to do this project over a garbage bag spread out on a hard floor. When you're done, scoop it all up and throw it away for a quick cleanup.

- *Large-motor skills* improve rapidly during this year. Giving your child time to chase after a large rubber ball, slide down a junior-size slide, or rock on a toddler-size rocking horse allows your little one to release some energy and practice those newly found large-motor skills.

- The fun of *reading* to your child can skyrocket at this age. Go to the library with a tote bag and fill it up. Read the stories. Act some of them out together. Have your child point out things you ask him or her to find in the pictures—a tree, a pig, a house, and so on. Help your child find and name colors. Use fun accents and noises—have a blast! You are instilling a love of reading that will last a lifetime.

Helpful hint: As this year goes on, you may notice that your child wants something you don't want him or her to have or something someone else is using. Before engaging a power struggle that will result in a meltdown, try finding something else to enthusiastically offer your child in order to distract him or her. Then discreetly remove the object from your child's line of sight (while breathing a well-earned sigh of relief).

Feeding

Although the twelve- to twenty-four-month-old is getting the vast majority of his nutrition from solids, consider what we wrote about how children at this age still speak the language of touch and sensation while they are developing their basic linguistic abilities. Nutritionally, breast milk changes as the nursing child gets older and continues to be good brain food.[1] That's why the American Academy of Pediatrics states that nursing should continue well beyond the first year of life if possible, that the child continues to receive significant nutritional and health benefits from nursing past the first year, and that there is no upper limit to the nursing relationship or evidence that nursing into the third year or even longer is harmful psychologically or in any other way.[2] The fact is that God designed the child's body to still seek Mommy for milk even after her nutritional needs can be met in other ways. Healthwise, children nursed past the first year have more antibodies to fight infection than weaned children and get sick less often and for shorter durations. Nursing has social benefits to the child as well. For instance, we know that a toddler's main occupation—taking independence—proceeds best when the child has a secure base of operations from which to launch. Knowing that Mommy is there with all the things that most comfort her is a tremendous relief to a child who is constantly testing boundaries and taking on new challenges.

Extended nursing is good for Mommy too. Nursing for at least a year has been shown to cause a decreased risk of breast cancer, ovarian cancer, rheumatoid arthritis, high blood pressure, heart disease, and diabetes; and the longer you nurse, the lower your risk for these diseases goes.[3] More immediately, on a busy day when your little one is running circles around you, it's nice to know that you still have a way to convince him to sit still. As we share in chapter 8, this is a great way to continue reading aloud to your child, fostering an early love of learning. Listening to the way God designed the child's body to function best may be countercultural, but it pays huge dividends in the form of a happier, healthier toddler and a happier mom too.

> **Lisa:** Contrary to what people might think, I'm really not the "Earth Mother" type. But I loved nursing my toddlers. There's nothing like that grateful smile when your busy little wonder snuggles up, nurses, and plays with your face and hair. I love reading to my kids, and I took full advantage of their nursing time to read to them. They ate it up, literally! It was so nice to have a ready way to get an active toddler to settle and just stay still for even a few minutes. When I saw other moms pulling their hair out trying to get a break from a toddler who never wanted to stop, it made me so grateful for my extended nursing relationship with my little ones. I understand the motivation for weaning by or after the first year, but in my experience, it just makes everything more stressful and more complicated in the long run. I wanted my parenting life to be as simple and care-free as possible. Extended nursing helped make that a reality for the toddler years.

If you haven't stopped nursing by the time your child is a year or more, consider extending it for as long as you and your little one get something out of it. The World Health

Organization reports that breast milk continues to be an important source of nutrition and energy through at least twenty-four months and the source of ongoing psychological comfort beyond that.[4] The world average for nursing is five years, and while we are not expecting you to do this, you need to understand that nursing in some limited way until your baby is at least three is actually healthy and recommended by the majority of the world's doctors and moms alike.[5] You certainly don't need to make a show or a crusade of it. By this time, because your child doesn't depend on nursing for his sole nutrition, you don't even need to do it out of the house if you don't like. But there is nothing wrong—and a lot that's pretty wonderful—about stealing a few special, quiet moments with your toddler—even an older toddler—to remind each other that despite all the new and exciting places there are to explore, home is in Mom's lap. And there is no place like home.

Sleep

Once again, don't feel that you need to be in a rush to move your twelve- to twenty-four-month-old out of your room or even out of your bed. At this age, your child still does not have any significant self-comforting ability. Some children are just fine moving out at this stage and others are not, but all kids take their independence eventually. Trust yours to do so as well. This age is challenging because the way an eighteen-month-old thinks about being away from Mom is different from how a twelve-month-old thinks about being away from Mom. Ironically, the older toddler is actually more fearful of being away from Mom. In the earlier months, the child is still fairly certain that he is connected to Mom at least in some way, and so he feels a little more secure.

Many parents try and even succeed in moving their child to a separate sleeping space at this age only to find that the child is incessantly coming back to bed only a few months later. This is not a discipline problem. It is a simple effect of your child's maturing brain. By about eighteen months to twenty-four months, your toddler has finally figured out for sure that you and he really are two different people. That can be a bit of a shock. Think of it. Everything you thought you knew about yourself and the world turns out not to be true. Who wouldn't need a little reassurance?!? We understand when parents complain about their successfully transitioned children's return to their bed. From Mom and Dad's point of view, it looks like failure on their part or a regression on their baby's part. But it's not. It's just your little one growing up and needing your reassuring presence while she does it. She is only responding as God created her body to respond. If you can be gentle and understanding about this, it will all go better in the long run. We recommend not putting pressure on yourself or your toddler to sleep separately until your child demonstrates that she is ready. For dealing with your questions about sleep, we cannot recommend highly enough Elizabeth Pantley's excellent book *The No-Cry Sleep Solution for Toddlers and Preschoolers*,[6] along with her entire No-Cry series of books.

Psychosocial Milestones

The joy of two-legged exploration from twelve to eighteen months can often give way to some degree of anxiety from eighteen to twenty-four months. As we indicated in the section on sleep, that's because the toddler has finally figured out that you're really and truly two separate people. *Well, I'll be!* For some little ones, this is a bit of a shock to the system, and the child who was constantly running off by himself now suddenly doesn't want to leave your side. Nothing's wrong. He just needs to be sure you are still going to be there. This, by the way, is another reason extended nursing is such a terrific idea. Too many parents are lulled into a false sense of confidence thinking that their young toddler doesn't want or need them the same way anymore, so they wean. Then, four to six months later, when the toddler hits the eighteen- to twenty-month mark, they find they've eliminated the very thing that would have set their little one's world right again—that is, a little time reminiscing at Mom's breast, remembering what it felt like in those bygone days when Baby and Mommy were completely one and life was simple and we didn't have to be so darned independent and explore-y all the time.

Language Milestones

Your baby will spend this second year of life focusing on learning a new language of words and signs (i.e., tones of voice and gestures that change the meaning of words) that will eventually replace the old language of touch and cuddles. For now, your little one is still most familiar with the language of affection. By about eighteen months, your baby should probably be able to say a handful of single words, and by twenty-four months, your little one will most likely be able to put words together into two- to three-word phrases. Also, at around twenty-four months, your toddler will begin responding to two-part commands, like "Please pick up your toy and hand it to me."

As we suggested in chapter 8, you cannot read to your child too early or too often. Twelve to twenty-four months is an especially good time to be reading short picture books to your child. Some parents complain that their little one won't sit still for a story. This is another good reason for those moms who are able and willing to remember the benefits of extended nursing. Nursing gives you more opportunities to convince your toddler to sit still and listen to you read! Regardless, even if your little one refuses to stay still during story time no matter what, it's okay. Toddlers still benefit from hearing you read to them while they are crawling, scooting, walking, or even running about. Call your little one over to see the pictures. He'll get a kick out of meandering over to look at the new exciting image you've found for him to look at.

Potty Training

Most parents can't wait until their kids are out of diapers. The end of the expense and mess can't come soon enough. But there is no point rushing it. Early control of the sphincter muscles that allow your child to control elimination begins at eighteen months or so. We focus more on actual potty-training strategies in chapter 16. For now, it's enough to know that it's coming. It would be okay to purchase a training potty or potty seat for your child at this time. Even if you don't use it a lot, your child will probably love sitting on his or her potty chair with a good book, just like Mom and Dad, because children this age love to imitate grown-ups.

The theme across the common developmental milestones of early toddlerhood continues to be "relax and trust God." Obviously, if you feel that your child is not hitting the milestones we described, you should consult with your pediatrician. But in general, the best strategy is just to trust the programming God hard-wired into your child's body. You can certainly encourage walking and talking and potty training and all the other skills your young toddler is beginning to learn in earnest, but resist the temptation to force them. Don't feel like a failure if your baby isn't catching on as quickly as your sister's genius baby or think that your little one is being defiant if she isn't ready to sleep alone. Her brain is still developing. Give it the time it needs to prepare to do this most important work.

Healthy Toddler Discipline

Oddly enough, the day before we sat down to write this chapter, we got an e-mail from a listener to our radio program, *More2Life*, which we want to share with you.

> Hello Dr. Greg and Lisa,
>
> I would like to ask you something, if you can help me. I have a baby who is 14 months old. My husband thinks the baby needs to be disciplined in everything he does. If the baby reaches for a plant he puts the baby in time out. If the baby goes behind the couch he puts the baby in time out. Today, because our baby reached out to touch one of our living room plants, he held our son until he cried saying, "He needed a time out." He held our baby for the time-out because, even though we usually use a crib, we were at my mother-in-law's and we didn't have it with us.
>
> Beyond this, my husband even wants to correct the baby when the baby is crying or tired. If I tell him he is being too hard on our child, my husband starts telling me if my baby

becomes a delinquent it will be my fault. Who's right?

Maria

Parents of toddlers in general, and first-time parents especially, often make the mistake of thinking that a walking child is a big kid with big-kid abilities like self-control and reason. They see their child delight in touching things they shouldn't touch and assume that the child is being "willful," intentional, and even conniving. It can certainly seem that way when we see our baby's actions through adult eyes, but it is not at all what Baby is doing. When a child keeps insistently returning to something we have told them they shouldn't touch, an adult thinks, "That child is being defiant! I must stop him now or he is going to grow up to be a serial killer, and my picture will be on the news with the caption 'Serial Killer's Parents: They Never Said No!'" We think this way because a desire to be defiant is the only reason we—with our fully formed adult brains—would knowingly, consistently, and intentionally keep doing something someone we care about has directly told us not to do. But that's how *we* think.

Toddlers Are Not Defiant

What a young toddler *actually* thinks when he repeatedly goes near something he has been told not to touch is "That looks interesting! I NEED to get a closer look at that! Also, when I go near it, that big one goes 'BLAH-BLAH-BLAH-BLAH!' Ha! *That's* funny! I want to see that again!"

Despite what many people believe—and despite how it may feel to experience toddler behavior as an adult—toddlers are not defiant. Why would they be? It makes no sense. They are utterly, completely, and totally dependent upon you for survival. Why would they intentionally want to infuriate you, to drive you from them or bring out feelings in you that make you want to harm them? Some Catholic parents answer that question with "original sin." While it's true that *concupis-cence* (the longing for the mud that remains after Baptism has washed clean the stain of original sin) makes it hard for us to know the right way to satisfy our desires, concupiscence isn't sin. It isn't defiance either. It's just simple ignorance, confusion, and an unrestrained curiosity, and toddlers have cornered the market on these qualities. In fact, these qualities are what you might call the top three occupational hazards of being a toddler—a little human with a brain that is only half-formed.

Before the Fall, humans were perfectly united with God. John Paul II taught that this means that all of our desires and passions were properly ordered as well. Because our relationship with God was intact, arguably our internal sense of the best way to meet our needs was also fine-tuned, and it propelled us toward healthy things. After the Fall, not so much. We still have our passions and our desires that bubble up from our lower, childish brain, but the spiritual connection that showed us how to meet them in a godly way was severed by original sin. Jesus's passion, death, and resurrection restored the connection, but only to the degree that we can hear God somewhat more clearly. The connection won't be totally healed until we are one with God in heaven. In the meantime, we are stuck working with a present but not yet completely healed connection to the heavenly graces we need to manage our passions easily and well.

God Calls Us to Have Mercy

And what is God's response to our condition? The same one he wants parents to have: *mercy* (Mt 18:21–35). God recognizes that it is hard for us to know and do what is right and good and proper, and so he mercifully leads and guides us to the truth, and asks us to do the same for our children.

Our point is that your young toddler will do many, many, stupid, frustrating things that can seem defiant, but they are not. Toddlers are just little people with half-formed brains and a fritzy human connection to God that prevents them from knowing how all these feelings and desires they're having should be properly managed. So, maybe we should give them a little break?

In our book *Beyond the Birds and the Bees*, we discuss what it takes to form a virtuous, moral child from toddlerhood through young adulthood.[1] Brain scientists who study the development of what could be called "the moral brain" tell us that the structures of the brain that are concerned with moral decision making and empathy (the ability to intimately feel the effect my actions have on you, an essential quality in moral reasoning) grow best in a family environment that favors extravagant affection and a gentle, consistent approach to discipline that emphasizes clear rules and high expectations coupled with repetitive practice and patient instruction in what psychologists call the *positive opposite*.[2] The positive opposite is just a fancy way of saying that we should spend about a thousand times more energy redirecting and teaching our children what they *can* do and what we would prefer them to do than we spend on yelling at them, punishing them, and shaming them for what they did wrong.

Discipline in the Catholic Tradition

Despite the horror stories you may have heard from grandparents and the urban legends about Catholic education by angry nuns before the Second Vatican Council, Catholic saints have almost universally counseled gentle approaches to discipline for all children, regardless of their age, since the earliest days of Christianity.

St. John Chrysostom (AD 347–419), whose teachings were so influential to the development of the Christian faith that he was given the title "Doctor of the Church," counseled fourth-century Christian parents to *"accustom your child not to be trained by the rod; for if he feels it . . . he will learn to despise it.*

And when he has learnt to despise it, he has reduced thy system to naught."[3]

St. Jean-Baptiste de la Salle, who founded the Institute of the Brothers of the Christian Schools in the late 1600s, wrote, *"The birch is used only out of bad temper and weakness, for the birch is a servile punishment which degrades the soul even when it corrects, if it indeed corrects, for its usual effect is to burden."*[4]

Writing in the 1800s, St. John Bosco, who was known for his effectiveness in reforming even the most hardened juvenile delinquents, wrote what he called "The Preventive System" of education and parenting, which counseled:

> Force, indeed, punishes guilt but does not heal the guilty. . . . Praise of work well done and blame in the case of carelessness are already a great reward or punishment. A reproachful or severe look often serves as an excellent means of moral restraint over the young. By it the guilty person is moved to consider his own fault, to feel ashamed, and finally to repent and turn over a new leaf. Never, except in very extreme cases, expose the culprit publicly to shame. . . . The greatest prudence and patience should be used to bring the [child] to see his fault, with the aid of reason and religion. To strike a child in any way . . . must be absolutely avoided. . . . [These punishments] greatly irritate the child and degrade the [authority figure].[5]

Catholic leaders have been counseling restraint, patience, and gentility for parents since the earliest days of the Church. Psychology, brain science, and our Catholic faith agree that children learn best when we as parents can assume a positive intention behind our children's misbehavior, gently correct the wrongdoing, and redirect the child toward what he or she should be doing instead. Toddler discipline, in particular, should absolutely not involve harsh consequences or punishments. Time-outs, spanking, and taking away toys are all completely useless. Toddler brains can't make sense out of these consequences. At best they make the parent feel useful without actually being useful to anyone—least of all the toddler. And the more you cling to these inappropriate, albeit well-intentioned, means of correcting your toddler, the more of a monster toddler you will create. That is likely to convince you that you need to do even more bad parenting, which will lead to an even more poorly behaved child, and so on and so on. And that *is* how you raise an axe murderer.

Teaching Self-Regulation and Self-Control

The goal of "discipline" at this stage is not so much teaching good behavior. Rather, it is laying the groundwork for self-regulation and self-control. *Self-regulation* refers to the ability to master overwhelming emotions, including the emotional impulse to do things one is not permitted to do. *Self-control* refers not only to the ability to "not" do certain things but also to the ability to figure out what to do instead. Your child will not actually master these skills for several years, but he can develop them sooner rather than later if you use more gentle approaches to correction. The more heavy-handed parents are, the longer it takes for a child to learn self-regulation and self-control. Regardless, the focus of your interactions around your child's misbehavior at this age should be establishing that you are the person whose job it is to help him calm down and focus on what he can do when he has been doing something he shouldn't. These are terrifically important skills. All of us need someone to turn to when we have a hard time calming down and figuring out what to do. Children under twelve months tend naturally to turn to Mom and Dad to help them calm down and get back on line, but this is not always true for the budding toddler, whose motto is "Do by SELF!" Sometimes, our little ones need us to remind them that we are their best resource for restoring their sense of internal peace and well-being. Once children develop *self-talk* (the internal voice we all use to regulate our emotional reactions) between the ages of four and six, they can be given more responsibility for working out their emotions. Until then, it will be helpful to turn toward Mom and Dad. This is the time to teach the foundation for self-regulation and self-control. If you fail to use the toddler years to lay this foundation and focus instead on compliance, you will spend years playing catch-up, trying to make your child learn to calm down and listen to you. Trust us, you don't want that.

The Three Rs of Toddler Discipline

So what can you do? Use the three Rs of toddler discipline: *reposition, redirect,* and *reregulate.*

Reposition

This means put stuff away. If a toddler shouldn't be near it, put it away, baby-proof it, cover it up, and/or block access to it. This parenting technique is brought to you straight from the Lord's Prayer.

Every time we say the Our Father, we pray, "and lead us not into temptation" (Mt 6:13). How can we expect our heavenly Father to hear our prayer if we won't extend this courtesy to our toddlers? Remember, "Whatever you did for one of these brothers of mine, you did for me" (Mt 25:31–46) and "Whoever causes one of these little ones who believe in me to sin, it would be better for him to have a great millstone hung around his neck and to be drowned in the depths of the sea" (Mt 18:6). It strikes us as a tremendous abuse of God's generosity to accept his mercy for ourselves and then set our toddlers up to fail. If you have a toddler in the house, put the off-limits thing away, cover it up, block access to it, or make your peace with the fact that your toddler is going to do what toddlers do best—explore the dickens out of it from the inside out. Your child is a little explorer. If you don't want something to be explored, take it off the map. Don't lead your toddler into temptation.

Redirect

If your toddler wants to do something and you don't want him to, redirect him to something else. But here's the trick: it's all about your sales pitch. If your toddler is running toward the delicate plant behind the couch (to use our correspondent's example), don't mutter, "Hey. How 'bout playing with Mr. Bunny. Want bunny?" Instead, you need to say, "WOW! Look at Mr. BUNNY! He's SO HAPPY! What's that, Mr. Bunny? You want to tell Timmy something? You DO? Here you go TIMMY! Want Mr. Bunny?" You have to sell it if you want your kid to buy it. Otherwise, regardless of what Lassie says about it, Timmy's going to end up in the well . . . again.

Reregulate

We know they look all grown up walking around like that, but no matter how much swagger junior's managing to generate, his parasympathetic (calm-down) nervous system is still not developed enough to help him calm down if he gets upset or frustrated. That means he's going to tantrum . . . a lot.

Isn't a tantrum defiance? No. According to Margot Sunderland in *The Science of Parenting*, there are two types of tantrums: "distress tantrums" and "Little Nero tantrums." Little Nero tantrums are the manipulative, defiant tantrums, and they tend to happen in children older than four or five who have some beginnings of self-control and some capacity for self-talk. By contrast, distress tantrums are exactly what they sound like. They are signs that the toddler's internal stress management systems are completely overloaded because he is tired, hungry, overwhelmed, or frustrated.[6]

Toddlers spend a lot of time being frustrated. In our book *Parenting with Grace*, we suggest that the best way to understand the inner life of the toddler is to imagine being a stroke victim (God forbid).[7] Imagine being able to see yourself doing any number of things expertly or forming any number of words perfectly, but finding yourself unable when you make the attempt. Over and over again, your best efforts to accomplish tasks or say what you need to say are frustrated and wrecked. And to top it all off, every time you get out of your hospital bed to try to test your legs, you have a nurse yelling "Don't do this! Don't do that!" at you. Pretty vexing, right? Welcome to toddlerhood!

Because the toddler has so many frustrations to contend with and so few brain systems to manage them, he needs you to help him calm down. Incidentally, this is not a design flaw. The Theology of the Body tells us that we were made for connection, and God's design of the body bears this out. Your toddler having a distress tantrum doesn't need a time-out. He needs *time-in* to help him reregulate. He needs to be held close to your body, soothed, and talked to gently so that your comforting rituals can stimulate his vagus nerve to get him calmed down and back on line. Now, time-in often isn't cuddly and love-y. It is often more like wrestling a greased manatee. Don't let your child kick, smack, or head-butt you. You can hold your child as firmly as you need to in order to prevent such behaviors. Holding time works best for the under three set. If you start time-in early enough, most kids have pretty good self-control by three or four, so the long-term payoff is worth it.

Parents often ask, "But doesn't all that physical affection just reward bad behavior?" It would if you were cuddling a kid who was having a Little Nero tantrum (that's who time-outs are for), but kids under three and certainly babies from twelve to twenty-four months are not neurologically capable of Little Nero tantrums. When you give your child time-in, you are actually stimulating the parts of his brain that will help him deal with stress more effectively later, thus giving him the skills he needs to handle life better. God wants your child to need you intimately in the first three years of life. If you can accept this, you and your child will be happier and healthier for the effort.

Toddler discipline is very simple and very repetitive. Just remember the three Rs of *reposition, redirect,* and *reregulate,* and do them over and over and over again. *Reposition* tempting items. *Redirect* your child away from things you don't want her to touch to things you do want her to touch (and SELL IT!). *Reregulate* your toddler's stress response (i.e., distress tantrums) with *time-in* (firm but loving physical connection that stimulates his "calm-down" brain). That is the sum total of disciplining your twelve- to twenty-four-month-old. Any more than this is ineffective overkill. Work with God's design of your child's brain and body, and you will help your child be hard-wired for virtue throughout life.

CHAPTER FOURTEEN

Turning the Corner

Mom Care

Making it through your first year is a huge milestone. Congratulations! You deserve to feel great about yourself. You've gotten both you and your baby through tons of "firsts": first teeth, first holidays, perhaps even a first word or first step, and so much more. You have become the expert on your baby, and you're probably starting to recapture a sense of yourself again too.

The second year, of course, brings new challenges along with new joys. One of the biggest challenges is how to take care of yourself, as your baby starts to move at light speed through his day, while continuing to bond with him. Over the next few months, you'll probably find that your baby is becoming more and more fun to be with. Even so, this can also be a time when you start feeling a little bit crazy from only reading books with one-syllable words and listening to children's songs that never leave your head, especially if you are a stay-at-home mom. The first section of this chapter focuses primarily on managing time at home with your baby, and then we offer some additional consideration for moms who work outside the home.

Managing Time at Home with Baby

Regardless of whether you are home full time or working out of the house at least some of the time, the key to keeping sane at this stage is to enjoy your child to the fullest. We've talked about the importance of routines and rituals throughout the book, and this is an age when it is especially important to be intentional about the rhythm of your day. Having more or less regular times and ways of doing breakfast, art time, playtime, lunch, nap, music time, outdoor time, and story time gives your child the predictability he needs to stay emotionally regulated and engaged with you. Having a rhythm to your day makes it possible for you to carve out some time for yourself.

Eat Well

Make sure you eat well at meals and snack times. Resist the temptation to graze scraps off your toddler's plate. A recent study in the *American Journal of Clinical Nutrition* shows that you can take in an extra, and unnecessary, 1500 calories or more a day just by eating scraps off your child's plate on your way to the garbage can. Don't treat yourself like a garbage can. If you stumble over wasting food, rethink and rework what and how much you are offering your child. Sometimes less is more, knowing you can add a bit more after the first offering is successfully eaten.

Feed Your Brain

Always have three different books that you alternate among to feed your mind. Don't worry about reading them all the way through in any kind of efficient manner. Just having them at the ready so you can dip in and read when you get a spare moment is a great way of fending off maternal brain rot. The first book should be something fun that you can read as an escape. Let your second book be a nonfiction title about some area of interest to you (e.g., culture, fashion, music, history, politics, science, etc.). Let the third book be something related to spiritual enrichment: a bible study, a devotional, lives of the saints, etc. Even reading a paragraph a day in at least one of these books helps you feel that you are maintaining your mind and spirit and that you have something to contribute in conversation with other adults.

Manage Your Media

When you are home with your child, be intentional about what you listen to. Grab your news off the Internet, don't have it piped into your minds by leaving the television on all day. Leaving on the television in general can overstimulate toddlers, and leaving on the news in particular can frighten your child and increase your own sense of anxiety as well, as you keep tuning in to get the update on the latest crisis. In 2011 the American Academy of Pediatrics (AAP) issued its second caution to parents (the first was in 1999) about letting children under two watch television, including both *secondhand television* (adult programming that babies incidentally tune in to when Mom and Dad are watching) and children's programming. The report notes that there is no evidence that videos and television programs for children under two are helpful at all, and there is good reason to suggest they may be harmful to developing brains, negatively affecting attention span and impulse control.[1]

We recognize that, as the *New York Times* noted, 90 percent of parents will let their infants watch television and that in our hyperwired world it is next to impossible—and even unnecessary—to *completely* eliminate television from your baby's life.[2] That said, we recommend adopting a mindful and intentional attitude toward television viewing. In other words, unless you are intentionally watching something you particularly enjoy, the television should be off.

Instead, make music front and center in your house. In addition to regular music time with your toddler, make sure that you have your MP3 or CD player stocked with some good praise and worship, classical, jazz, or other upbeat tunes with family-appropriate lyrics to keep stimulating your mind and mood.

Exercise Creatively

Make sure you get some exercise every day with your toddler. You don't have to take an expensive class (although there are many wonderful mommy-toddler exercise classes offered that may allow you to socialize with other moms). A daily walk, some dancing with your little one, or a mommy-toddler exercise DVD can serve to get you moving and feeling like you're doing something for you while still building rapport with your child.

Socialize Mindfully

Most moms crave some manner of socializing, but choose your social supports wisely. That goes double for any Internet relationships or groups you belong to (more on this in a moment). Make sure the people you get your "grown-up time" with support your relationship with your child. If they are always encouraging you to go out and get some me-time, or to leave your spouse and kids for a girls' weekend away, try to limit those relationships to occasional get-togethers. While some time away from your child can be a lifesaver, be sensitive to how much time you spend away from your child. Even at this age, the more time you spend away from your child, the harder it is to pick up on your child's cues and maintain the level of relationship that establishes you in your child's mind as a secure base. Too much advice of this kind will begin to deplete you and possibly make you question the importance of your parenting role.

Communicate with Your Husband

Make sure you're giving your husband the opportunity to get alone time with your toddler, but turn over to your husband a well-rested and well-fed little person at times that can be successful. As much as possible, avoid the game of "Tag, You're It," handing the baby off to your husband the moment he comes through the door. This has less to do with respecting your husband than it does with not setting your husband and baby up for failure. Handing a tired, hungry toddler off to a tired, hungry husband as a melting-down mom runs out the door like it's the escape hatch on a crashing plane is a recipe for disaster. Instead, we recommend using that after-work time to connect as a family—support each other through your collective hunger and tiredness by getting dinner to the table together, catch up, and take turns playing with your toddler while he gets oriented to having Dad home again. Once you have worked with your husband and child together to make sure that everyone is fed and has had time to regroup and reconnect, then you can take some time for yourself. Now you won't be worried that your husband will call after five minutes asking you how to handle a hysterical child or that, after getting your time to unwind, you're going to just get wound up again because you're coming home to a house full of grumpy people.

Temper Internet Time

It can be easy to let an entire day slip away with us staring at our smartphone, tablet, or computer instead of our little one. We all crave connection and can't always get out, so it's easy to convince ourselves that we are "right there" with our kids when really we're 10,000 miles away arguing with an old college friend about parenting practices instead of actually parenting.

While checking our smartphones can seem less intrusive than the television or the telephone, it still presents a huge distraction from parenting. In fact, it's becoming a huge child safety and health risk. Emergency room physicians are reporting a significant rise in injuries to children whose parents were physically present but distracted by digital media. In the first three years after smartphones hit the market, pediatric visits to the emergency room increased by 12 percent, reversing the downward trend in pediatric ER visits since the 1970s.[3]

The Catholic layperson is called to ask him- or herself, "How can I bring a little more of myself, of God's love, and of my heart to this task?" When we think of holy people, we often think in cartoony terms of people who glow in the dark or bilocate. But that's not the mark of holiness. If you think of actual holy people such as Mother Teresa, John Paul II, or Pope Francis, the one thing that the people who encountered them always claim is that even if they were in a crowd of thousands, for the moment that they were with one of these holy people, they felt like they were the only person in the world. One of the signs of holiness is *presence*, the ability to be right here, right now and make the person you are with feel like they are the most important thing.

We're all works in progress. Maybe someday people will say the same thing about us that they say about the holy men and women we mentioned above, but for now, all we can do is try to pull ourselves away from the screens and be as present to our spouses and children as possible. There will be plenty of other people telling our kids throughout their lifetime that they don't really matter all that much or that they matter less than this or that. As parents, let's strive to counter this message, not by bombing our children with empty praise, but by turning away from the distractions, being present, and appreciating the gift they are to us.

The more you can be present, the more you will be able to experience the opportunities for holiness hidden in the little moments between you and your child, the better socialized your child will be, and the less you will feel that you spend your day trapped in "Kiddieland." Even at this age, a

well-supervised child who has been taught to thrive on interaction with attentive parents can go to museums, concerts in
the park, and even decent restaurants and other places with a
little prior planning.

If You Work Outside the Home

If you are pulling double-duty working outside the home all
day and then spending time with your child and husband at
night and on weekends, mom care may seem like an impossible dream, and in many ways, it is. The fact is, when you are
already spending most days away from your child, more time
away from your child for girls' night out and me-time isn't
going to serve you or your family well. So what's an exhausted
mom to do?

Be aware that you and your child will often be in a state of
dysregulation simply because you spend your days apart with
different schedules and a different pace. When parents and
children are in this state of dysregulation, it can be natural to
just start pushing each other away because being together feels
"off" somehow. This isn't catastrophic. It is just something to be
aware of and attentive to. The best mom care you can do is to
focus on getting back in synch with your child in the evenings
and on weekends. That's what makes your relationship with
your child feel easier and more pleasant and helps boost your
confidence as an effective, connected mom. All of that goes a
long way to beat back the guilt many working moms feel about
not being able to be there as much as they might otherwise like.
Here are some ways to make that happen.

Recollect Your Child after Work

Even though you are probably dying to pick up your child
from the caregiver, run your errands, get home, fix dinner,
bathe your baby, get him to sleep and collapse, make sure to
plan to pause at the caregiver's. Spend at least five to ten minutes with your child in "his" space. Find out what his day

was like from the caregiver. Sit on the floor and let him and his friends play around you (first) and with you (once he feels recollected) for a few minutes. When you feel your relationship click back into place, it's time to go.

On the drive home, turn off your cell phone and talk to your child in simple sentences about his day and what the evening ahead is going to be like. He will not understand everything you are saying at first, but he knows you are engaging with him and, in time, he will come to understand and appreciate this little preparation for coming home, and your expectations will be in synch.

Make Nightly Connection

Do your best to plan one activity a night with your child. It can be as short as ten or fifteen minutes at this age, but do something fun (for some suggestions, see the activities we list at the beginning of part four). It is important to not let yourself be reduced in your child's mind to "the one who's busy all the time" or "the one who rushes me through meals/bath/bed." We're not saying any of this to make you feel guilty. It's just to help you see things through your child's eyes. He has been with someone else all day who has been providing for his needs and entertaining him. These activities have been building attachment between your child and his daytime caregiver, but he doesn't know what your role is and how to interact with you unless you teach him. Taking time to do a limited but fun activity each evening (and preferably doing it as a family) builds the rapport you need to stay connected and maintain the emotional regulation between the two of you.

It doesn't have to be a big deal or difficult. Make it easy on yourself. For instance, spread a couple of fresh garbage bags on the bathroom floor and put out some paper and finger paints. All of you can paint, play, and laugh together. Then one parent can draw the bath while the other hangs your masterpieces, puts away the paint and throws away the garbage bags for a quick cleanup! Playing with blocks, trains, toy animals—all the classics—allows you to spend imaginative time with your child without electronics to distract you. Make sure you're sharing as much eye contact as possible while having fun together.

Take Full Advantage of Nighttime Parenting

Make your baby's bedtime routine as cozy and connecting as possible. When your child has been depending on someone else to meet his needs during the day, he needs to know that you are the one he can rely on at night. Rooming in with baby, or even continued bed sharing, can be an especially big help to the dual-career family. By being intentionally present to your child at night, responding promptly to his cries, and even allowing him to cuddle up to you in bed, you are creating a closeness that would simply not be possible if you were to adopt a more conventional approach to baby sleeping arrangements. Even as advocates of this approach, we are consistently surprised to see how much this kind of contact means to little ones. As adults, who speak that language of words and symbols, we tend to discount sleep time as "off-line" time. For little ones, however, who even at this age still primarily speak a language of touch and cuddles, nighttime parenting is a powerful way to deliver a big "I love you, I missed you, and I'm so glad to be back with you" message to each other.

Make Weekends Together Time

On weekends, the dual-working couple has so much to get done. Even so, putting the tyranny of chores in front of reconnection time can just lead to further dysregulation between you and your child. Remember, being in synch with Baby is about being in contact with Baby. The less contact you have with each other, the harder it is to decode each other's signals and habits, which leads to confusion and frustration for parents and Baby. Obviously you need to get your house cleaned and your errands run, but instead of just diving into chores on the weekends, try this instead.

Know your child's day-care schedule. At what times of the day does your child have stories, music, snack, play, lunch, and so on? Try your best to incorporate even brief versions of these activities into your weekend schedule at approximately the same time your child does them at day care. Get up around the same time that you usually do, but take a little more time for cuddles and reconnecting than you usually have time for. Throughout the day, alternate between doing a chore and then doing one of the above activities with your child. Mom might do a chore while Dad plays with Baby, then Dad does a chore while Mom does music time, and then Baby has lunch and takes a nap. Let the day flow between connecting with Baby and catching up on chores as fluidly as possible. It's your weekend, so be creative and have fun. Just try to keep some predictable structure in place to prevent dysregulation.

Take Time for Yourself

Of course, given how hard you're working and how much time you're giving to your little one, you need time for yourself too. Take full advantage of the times you are alone. For instance, load your MP3 player with books to listen to on your commute when you're not with your child. They will take you to a place outside the work/child-care cycle and feed your mind in ways music and news cannot.

Use your lunch break to get out of the office and be by yourself at least once or twice a week, even if that means sitting alone in your car looking at your favorite blogs. This is time you aren't taking away from your family or work. It's your time. Use it, and other times like it, well.

Make sure to take your own prayer time every day. It's okay if you pray while you cuddle with your baby in the morning or during the lunch hour for at least several minutes. Or, for that matter, the time when you lie down with your baby at night is a great time to prayer. Pray a Rosary or other devotion, or just talk to God in your own words. Afraid you'll fall asleep and miss the rest of your evening with your husband? Don't worry. Just tell your spouse when you would like him to come and wake you, or set your phone to vibrate next to you when you want to get up. Having gotten a little nap yourself, you'll have a lot more of yourself left to bring to your evening.

Of course, you can work with your husband to help each other get some alone time too. For instance, one of you might take the little one to the park Saturday morning so the other can sleep in. Or one of you can go to the gym in the morning and the other in the afternoon, giving you each a little workout time and a little time with your child.

There is no question that having a two-career family is harder work, but it is the new normal. Of course there will be challenges; the good news is that if you can keep in mind our advice in chapter 5 about creativity, consultation, and commitment, then with God's grace and your good efforts, you will be sure to find a way to meet your needs and the baby's.

CHAPTER FIFTEEN

Spiritual Care of Your Toddler

Taking Baby to Mass

Few things are more challenging than bringing a young toddler—or really any young child—to Mass. When the question of whether parents should even attempt this feat of spiritual daring was raised on our Patheos.com psychology and religion blog, *Faith on the Couch* (http://www.patheos.com/blogs/faithonthecouch/), it quickly became one of the most popular, and surprisingly controversial, topics on the Catholic Channel at Patheos.

Some well-meaning parents don't even bother to try bringing their infants and toddlers to Mass, reasoning that since the experience is intellectually lost on them, it is pointless to bring them. We recommend against this course of action. Education doesn't begin with intellectual understanding. The way the brain learns is similar to the way a computer saves data. In a computer, first you create a file and then you save documents to the file. In the brain, I "create a file" when I am allowed to experience things I cannot yet understand. This new experience creates a space in the brain that will later be filled with the "documents" that tell me how I am to behave if the experience happens again, why I have had the experience, and finally what the experience means. Taking your infant and toddler to Mass *consistently* (or, for that matter, exposing your child to any situation consistently) creates a family ritual that establishes the neurological "file" in your child's brain. This file, opened long before understanding ever takes place, establishes the fact that this is something your family will be doing regularly and begins the process of priming your child's brain to learn *how* to behave at Mass and, eventually, *what* it all means and *why* it is so important.

None of this is to say that your child can't learn all these things later on, and you are certainly free to do what you think is best. That said, why deprive your children—at any stage of their lives—of the grace they need to grow into young men and women of God. Here are a few things to consider as you face this challenging time in your child's spiritual life.

The Baptized Belong

As far as Catholics are concerned, babies are not merely tolerated: they have a canonical (i.e., according to Church law) right to be in church. If you are baptized, you belong. Although it is true that small children are not obliged to attend Mass until they reach the age of reason (around seven years old), this does not mean that small children shouldn't be permitted at Mass.

Be Mindful, Not Scrupulous

Many parents of young children are afraid that their children might be disruptive to other churchgoers. While parents should absolutely do all they reasonably can to gently and patiently mind their children at church, there's absolutely no reason for parents to be so scrupulous about their children's behavior that it causes them stress or anxiety. We offer here some practical suggestions for managing your child's behavior at Mass that will also help you stay calm and able to participate to a large degree. As you are reasonably thoughtful and attentive to your child, it's enough to know that you are welcome and have no reason to be overly concerned with disturbing other worshippers. One of the core themes of Catholic social teaching is the Call to Family, Community, and Participation.[1] Among the principles that cluster under this broad heading is the assertion that every Catholic is to support the mission of families to raise godly children. Failure to do so is a serious offense against both charity and the dignity of the family. Any Catholic who scowls at the attentive parent of a crying baby at church should repent as much and, we believe, will be called to account for their hardness of heart. "Whatever you did for one of these least . . . " (Mt 25:31–46).

The Rhythm of Mass

While we respect the intention behind it and appreciate that every parent may once in a while have a reason other than illness to not bring their child to Mass, it is our opinion that parents who consistently leave a child at home "until he is old enough" are being unjust regarding the child's religious education. As we noted previously, education begins unconsciously before it begins consciously. Your baby or toddler needs to be given the opportunity to learn the rhythm, sights, sounds, and smells of the Mass before he is conscious enough to *understand* the Mass. Spirituality is primarily a sensory call (from God) that leads to a transformative response.[2] Robbing a child of that early sensory experience of God and his Church is a serious impediment to future catechesis and spiritual development.

Fussing versus Crying

There is a huge difference between a fussing baby and a screaming baby. As a matter of courtesy to the other worshippers, parents should always remove a child who is being loud and cannot be consoled after about a minute or so. That noted, everyone else around the family with the fussy child has an obligation to either put on an understanding, sympathetic smile or pretend not to notice and trust that the parent will handle it. As Jesus said to the apostles who were pushing the kids away, "get over your bad selves" (or something like that) (Mt 19:14). As a Church, we do not believe in contraception, and we certainly should not be promoting contraceptive sanctuaries.

Here are some tips on how to begin to teach your little one to behave in church and how to get more out of the experience of bringing your child to Mass.

Managing Your Child's Behavior at Mass

- *Sit in the front (counterintuitive as it sounds).* Kids behave better when they can look at what's going on instead of the back of some other parishioner.

- *Don't ever just sit in the cry room from the start.* Although we understand and support their intended use, in practice, most cry rooms are from the devil. It's like Lord of the Flies Sunday School in there. Go in only if necessary and only for as long as you need to, and then head back to your pew. You and your child will get more out of the experience of Mass from the sanctuary.

- *If you have to remove your child from the sanctuary,* hold her the entire time you are in the cry room or the back of the church. DO NOT under any circumstances put her down. If you take the child out and put her down and play with her (or, God forbid, let her run around) you will teach her—through simple Pavlovian conditioning—that she *needs* to cry to get the fun times that happen when she forces you to leave the sanctuary. Let your child have a minimal amount of freedom of movement if he allows you to stay the pew, but none if he makes you leave the sanctuary. If a little one is really that out of control, he isn't able to calm himself down anyway (remember our discussion about the myth of self-soothing). If he makes you leave, by all means be loving, sympathetic, compassionate, and affectionate, but hold him the entire time and DO NOT PUT THE KID DOWN. When he's quiet, return to the pew.

- *By all means, for children younger than about four, bring some quiet, soft, preferably religiously themed toy-like things.* Please leave the video games, toy cars, and noisy toys at home. There are plenty of religiously themed quiet toys and activities that can be found with a simple Internet search. Purchase a small selection of these items and keep them in a special "going to Mass" bag that the child doesn't get to see unless you are in church. That will keep these activities special. Try to put these things away before the consecration. At the elevation, point to the host and whisper something like "Look at the miracle! Look at Jesus. Say, 'I love you Jesus!'"

- *Don't do Mass in shifts. Mass is for families.* When parents say they aren't "getting anything out of Mass" when they bring small children, they are missing the point. What you get out of Mass when you have small children is the joy of passing your faith on to them. That's what you signed up for when you became a Catholic parent. Yes, it can be tough, and yes, you may certainly do other things to get your spiritual needs met, but Sunday Mass is for your family. Go as a family.

Getting the Most Out of Mass with Your Toddler

- *Get there early, if possible.* We realize the difficulties with this, but do what you can to find a Mass time that enables you to get to church early. Try to give yourself at least ten minutes to get settled and calm down before Mass starts. If you can't get there early, then at least focus on keeping yourself calm regardless of what time you arrive. No one is grading you. We're just glad you're coming. Relax. Babies are terrific barometers of their parents' moods.

Your tension will actually cause your baby to fuss more. The less harried, hurried, and stressed you feel when Mass begins, the better your experience will be.

- *Read the Mass readings before you go.* You can use any number of publications to access these or read them online at the United States Conference of Catholic Bishops' website (http://www.usccb.org/bible/).

- *Make sure to participate as fully as you can.* Yes, it can be a challenge, but resist the temptation to just give up and spend your time bouncing the baby in the back of the church, checking your phone to see when it's all going to be over. Pray as much as you are able. Sing as much as you are able. When you have to attend to your child instead of what is going on at Mass, say something like this little prayer: "Lord Jesus, you said 'Let the little ones come to me.' I've brought my little one to you. Help us make the most of this time with you." God will bless you abundantly for bringing your child to him even if the experience is outwardly less than rewarding. Trust that God is doing a deeper work in you—a work of increasing your patience, generosity, and love.

- *Stay a few minutes after Mass.* Each of you takes a turn with the baby while the other parent gets a few minutes to pray. Trust us. The time you take would be the time you'd be sitting in your car waiting in line in the parking lot. You can make better use of this time by connecting with God and reminding yourself why you're doing all this.

The Eucharist is the "source and summit of our faith."[3] It is where we encounter Jesus up close and personal. To deprive ourselves or our children of the opportunity to be in his Eucharistic presence, worshipping with our community, is to deprive ourselves mightily. Jesus Christ is the same yesterday, today, and forever. It stands to reason that his attitude toward our children at Mass remains the same today as it was when he walked the earth, "Let the children come to me" (Mt 19:14).

Keeping Jesus' open heart for children in mind, we would like to leave you with one last thought. Namely, the goal of going to Mass with children is not merely getting through Mass with children. Sometimes that's the best we can do—and that's okay—but the real point in bringing our children to Mass is to foster an intimate, loving encounter with Christ. The best way to make this happen is to do whatever is necessary to a maintain as loving, calm, and affectionate a presence with your children at church as possible. Yes, getting to Mass on time is important and so is teaching your child to behave in Church. But even more important is giving your infant or toddler the physical sense that church is a place where he is loved and cuddled and cared for as much as—if not more—than at home.

Cardinal Timothy Dolan, Archbishop of New York, once shared with us his memory of attending church with his parents. He said that he attributed a good portion of his vocation to the priesthood from being together as a family at Mass, watching his mom and dad hold hands at church, witnessing the loving presence they shared with each other as well as with him and his siblings. As Cardinal Dolan's experience attests, giving your infants and toddlers a loving and engaged experience at church is the best way to give them a lifelong love of Christ and his Church. It is this catechesis of the heart that makes it possible for your children to experience church, not as something to be suffered through and endured, but rather as an intimate encounter with the loving God who made them and who calls them to know and follow him even at this very young age.

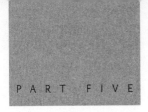

PART FIVE

The Year of Wonder

Twenty-Four to Thirty-Six Months

We are now solidly in toddlerhood and seeing your child's mind open up to the world around him or her. Chapter 16 looks at the developmental milestones of the twenty-four- to thirty-six-month-old. We look at one common mistake parents make, how to avoid it, and what you need to do to get the most out of this time in your child's life. We also look briefly at the development of the toddler discipline we began discussing in part four.

At this stage in their child's life, parents often begin asking themselves and each other when it might be time to consider having another child. Chapter 17 gives you some points to consider as you reflect on this important question. Finally, the book concludes with a chapter on resources to help you continue your journey toward becoming the best Catholic family you can be.

CHAPTER SIXTEEN

Enjoying the Terrific Twos

Although people often refer to it as the "terrible twos," the period from two to three years old can be a truly magical time. We like to think of it as a year of wonder. In our continuing quest to make parenting easier and your family life more enjoyable, we hope to offer some simple, practical ideas that can help you turn the terrible twos into the *terrific* twos.

We don't want to sugarcoat the fact that there can be many challenges in this coming year, but your child's intellect and abilities are growing by leaps and bounds and it can be a joy to experience. The two keys to success at this age are (1) being prepared for how active your child can be and (2) not overestimating your child's capabilities.

Be Prepared for Your Child's Developing Skills

This year, your child is going to become a master of movement. Those first, halting steps taken just a few weeks ago will quickly develop into running, climbing, jumping, and even walking backwards. The three Rs of toddler discipline still apply at this age, and *reposition* is one of them. It will be important to apply your baby-proofing strategies to areas that your child could not previously access.

Your child will also begin using simple sentences over the next few months. He'll be able to tell you when something hurts and where. Also, most children have resolved their confusion about how they can both be separate from you and still belong with you by this time. Most children at this age are less threatened by separation and can even use language to say where people are when they are not present (e.g., "Mommy is at work"). Children at this age begin to engage in symbolic and pretend play. They will start to name their toys. About midway through the year, most children begin displaying at least some interest in potty training, and about 98 percent of children will be potty trained by thirty-six months, at least for bowel movements. Urinary continence can take a bit longer, especially nighttime dryness. In short, your child will soon be giving you every indication that he or she is in the beginning stages of being a "big boy" or "big girl."

Don't Overestimate Your Child's Abilities

The continuing danger—especially for first-time parents—is that because your child is developing so many competencies, it is easy to think he is more grown up than he is. At this age, children's cognitive ability can be a source of endless fascination but can also be the source of a lot of confusion for parents because it is still fairly shallow. For instance, at this age children are still learning cause and effect. They are still delighted to realize that when they do something, a reaction follows—they just aren't necessarily sure that the same reaction will follow every single time. A child of this age will be thrilled to discover that when he pulls the dog's tail, the dog growls—this time. It is tremendous fun realizing that he can get a reaction—even out of you. It's just that the two-year-old hasn't yet learned that he will get a similar result every time he repeats the action. After all, this particular reaction was such an unexpected surprise, who's to say that the next time your child pulls the dog's tail, flowers might not sprout from its rear end? It's all such a tremendous mystery!

It is important for parents to remember their child's actual cognitive capability because you will be constantly frustrated if you don't. The answer to "*Why* did you pull the dog's tail *again*? You *know* what happened last time!" is, quite literally, "Because I was so surprised by what happened *last time* I wanted to see what *new thing* would happen if I did it again!" It will still be quite a while (until he is at least thirty-six months old) before the principle of cause and effect takes a firm hold of your child's brain and he stops wondering whether something new and exciting might happen each time he repeats some action.

Even though children of this age seem so much smarter than the baby you had just a few months ago, they have just enough intelligence to get themselves into trouble and too little to get back out. As such, toddlers of this age still need *constant* supervision.

Likewise, many parents think that now that their child is more verbal, they should see a decrease in tantrums. After all, as we noted previously, your baby can now tell you when she's hurting and where, right? The problem is that your child actually understands many more words than she can speak, and this will be the source of endless frustration for her. As we explained in chapter 13, your child is prone to tantrums because she can imagine doing so many more things with complete skill than her body is competent to execute! That's even truer now. Your toddler *knows* what she wants to say. She *knows* exactly what she wants to do. But no matter how hard she tries, the words just won't come out and the actions just won't come together. It's all so very frustrating!

We included the first three years in this book to emphasize that babyhood really extends through the entire first three years. Early childhood starts as your child finishes her third year, not before. We are not suggesting that you treat your child in a way that stifles his development, or that you somehow fail to encourage his maturation. You do, however, need to understand what is motivating your child's behavior—not so that you can excuse it, which would also be a mistake—but so that you can train her in a manner that respects God's design of her brain and body; that is, through gentle, consistent redirection and instruction on what to do.

In addition to being sensitively aware of the reality of your child's capabilities, here are some other important things you can do.

Don't Leave Your Toddler Unsupervised

This stage in the child's development is the time when many parents present to the emergency room with the phrase "I only turned my back for a minute!" From the perspective of brain science, toddlers are just babies who can move like the wind. Do not leave them unsupervised. When you need to do chores, bring your child with you. Take an extra moment to set him up with an activity in the space where you are working or give him a way to "help" you, but *do not* leave your child unattended. Many different abilities are emerging about which he needs your help to learn. The more present you can be, the fewer unpleasant surprises and "discipline issues" you will have.

Let Your Child Help You

Toddlers love to be given opportunities to "help" Mom and Dad.

> **Lisa:** When our little ones were toddlers, I would give them dust rags and tell them to follow after me as I cleaned, getting everything I missed. Obviously, I didn't miss anything that they would notice, and I certainly didn't actually expect them to dust! The point was that I needed to get something done and this was a way I could keep them busy and help

them develop their competence and sense of service. Each of our kids loved to be given big-girl or big-boy jobs to do. Children of this age begin to be able to sort things according to category (e.g., trucks are different than dolls). When I needed to fold socks, I would ask them to make a "dark pile" and a "light pile" or to help me find another sock with a similar pattern. Of course, 95 percent of their guesses were wrong. But we had great fun going back and forth with this helping game, and at regular intervals I would point out a sock that matched and say, "Does *that* sock go with *this* sock?" and then we'd celebrate when they brought it to me.

This is a great opportunity to begin teaching your child the virtue of *self-donation;* that is, the willingness to give of oneself in ways that make the lives of those around one easier or more pleasant. Kids are naturally fairly selfish. They want to learn how to be generous, but they don't know how to do it on their own. If you don't teach them now, it will be harder later on if they have learned that the best way they can help is to stay out of the way. Letting your child "help" is a great way to teach important skills like sorting, identifying colors, and organizing while training in the virtues of self-donation and generosity. It's a great way to get things done and be a good parent at the same time!

Read to Your Child

Hopefully, you have a well-established reading ritual with your child by now. If you have been practicing extended nursing and reading as we have suggested, your child is probably just as happy climbing up on your lap to read as he is climbing up for a quick nurse for comfort.

This is the time to read books that give your child an opportunity to interact with them. Pop-up books are great, as are books that replace certain words with pictures that allow your toddler to point to or even name the picture when it's his turn to help you "read" the sentence. The time from twenty-four to thirty-six months is as important for language development as the time from twelve to twenty-four months was for walking. This is the age when the more you can do to lay the groundwork for speech and communication, the better. That said, it should be fun time. Resist any urge to turn this into work by using word flash cards and the like. Any learning at this age should occur in a spirit of exploration and fun. Teach your child how to use her mind to explore and understand the wonder in the world around her. Reading together will open up new worlds of imagination for your child and will be inestimably helpful in facilitating your child's language development.

PLAYING WITH YOUR OLDER TODDLER

> We cannot fail to be witnesses of this joy.
> Christians are joyful, they are never gloomy.
> God is at our side.
>
> —POPE FRANCIS

This is an amazing time of play with your child. His or her imagination is almost infinite, which makes your child a blast to be with. All of the recommendations in part four still apply, but your child will bring even more imagination and capability to playtime.

- At this stage, it is important to balance both large- and small-motor play in your child's day. Give your child time to run, climb, and dance at intervals throughout the day. However, transition to recharging activities such as a snack, story time, or a small-motor sensory activity before your child gets exhausted and depletes his or her coping abilities.

- Continue the sensory play that your child was capable of from twelve to twenty-four months, but introduce more challenge, fun, and motor development by adding things like spoons, scoops, measuring cups, or training chopsticks to your sensory bins, so that your child can practice moving ingredients from one place to another. When provided with enough props, a child of this age can stay occupied with a sensory bin for quite a long time, with Mom or Dad just keeping a watchful eye. However, don't miss out on playing WITH your little one from time to time. It's really relaxing and fun in the midst of a stressful adult life.

- At this age kids love being in the kitchen with Mom and Dad. While of course we should keep them safely away from the hot and sharp elements of cooking, this is a great age to let kids start mixing and rolling batters and doughs. There are also wonderful child-safe knives on the market that allow your child to begin cutting veggies and fruit. Whether it's prepping for dinner or mixing up special recipes that become family traditions for holidays, cooking with your kids—even from this young age—is a wonderful way to teach skills, have fun together, and make memories that will last a lifetime.

- This is an appropriate age to play listening games with your child. Games like Simon Says or Freeze Dance (where your child dances to fun music and then freezes in place when you stop it) are amusing and help your child gain attention and direction-following skills.

- Blocks and construction toys are wonderful at this age. As your child gains more verbal capability, have her tell you stories about what she is building. It is wonderful to spend time inside your child's imagination, and she will love knowing you are taking the time to listen to what matters to her.

- Make-believe is awe inspiring at this age. Playing store, house, farm, etc., with your child isn't just fun; it can also bring you great hope as you daydream and pray for all your child may one day become.

Play at this age is wide open to the imagination, as long as you keep safety in mind. Unfortunately, many parents don't enjoy their children's play at this stage because there is just so much of it! Children of this age move from one thing to another very quickly and leave the materials they were playing with all over the place. This drives most of us crazy. So, note to us all, it's good to begin having your child help clean up one activity before moving on to the next. Sure, Mom and Dad will still need to do most of it, but if you use large, labeled bins, your two- to three-year-old can pick up toys and put them in the proper bin with your help and direction. It helps to do this in as fun a way as possible—with a song or a race. Remember Mary Poppins? If your child gives you a hard time, simply say, "Honey, will you put away your toys with me or do you want me to help you put away your toys?" If he continues to balk, gently but firmly take his little hand, pick up the toy together, lead him to the proper bin, and place the toy in it together. Then say, "Good, that's how you do it!" After two or three times, most children want to continue to help without you leading them through it.

With some creative organization (check websites like Pinterest for ideas if this is not your forte), you can keep your child's creativity within reasonable parameters so you can enjoy this wonderful, creative stage to the fullest.

Potty Training

The other major developing skill besides language that you will encounter this year is potty training. Many parents think of potty training as a discipline issue, but it is not. It is a developmental issue.

> **Greg:** I was more than happy to change diapers, but one experience in particular made me especially keen to get our kids potty trained as quickly as possible. I was in the middle of changing our baby's diaper (the child shall remain nameless to prevent public embarrassment). I had gotten the dirty diaper off and was lifting the child's legs to get the new diaper on when suddenly our little one had an attack of explosive diarrhea. I never knew that someone that little could generate so much poop with such incredible force. Of course, as I had just lifted the child's legs to get the diaper on, the point of origin for this shower of diarrhea was aiming directly at my face and, yes, my open mouth (I was singing to the baby at the time). I will never forget that experience. Not ever. I just stood there stunned. I'd been peed on before. That's bad enough. This was a whole new level of awful. Twenty years on, I still shudder to think of it. It was both the funniest and most traumatic moment of my fathering career. Oh, and lesson learned: Save the singing until after the fresh diaper is safely covering the region in question.

Regardless of our desires as parents, each child will come into being potty trained in his own time. There will be days when you doubt it will ever happen, but every child learns to control his bowels and bladder eventually. Your job is to provide patient encouragement and promote your child's awareness of his bodily signs by giving consistent feedback—for instance, "You're making your 'gotta go potty' face. Let's try!" or "I see you holding yourself. I think your body is saying, 'Let's use the potty!'"

You have been listening to and learning from God's design of your child's body since he was born. Now it's time to start teaching your child to listen to his body too. Potty training isn't just about making your child more convenient for you. It is about teaching him how to accommodate his behavior to the language of his own body. As he learns this skill with your encouragement, it will translate into other behaviors related to self-control such as eating when he's hungry and stopping when he's full, going to bed when he's tired, asking for a hug when he feels unsettled, or taking time to calm down when he's worked up. We don't mean to imply that if you get this wrong, all of these other behaviors are lost! Not at all. It's just important to understand the big picture and not get so focused on making your child potty proficient that you fail to realize that you are teaching other, lasting lessons about the importance of listening to one's body.

On average, girls potty train by twenty-nine months and boys by thirty-one months; most children aren't ready to begin trying to potty train until between twenty-four and twenty-seven months. In general, if you start any earlier, it just takes longer because your child's body is simply not ready to exhibit good bowel control before then. Again, potty training is not a matter of discipline. It is a matter of physiological readiness. Regardless, the time frames we indicate are just averages that mean little to you and your child. Each child is unique and unrepeatable and therefore deserves to be given the chance to grow at his or her own pace, as long as you are within the general framework of what is considered to be healthy.

According to the American Academy of Pediatrics, you'll know your child is ready to begin potty training when he begins showing signs that he is eager to please and wants to do more things by himself. Most important, of course, is that his bowel movements have begun occurring at mostly regular intervals and he is able to stay dry for a few hours at a time, including nap time. Starting before your child's body is ready is a fool's errand and likely to lead to terrific frustration and mistaking a developmental issue for a discipline issue. This is one of the worst things a parent can do, because the child can't possibly succeed at tasks his body is incapable of achieving.

Once your child's body is showing signs of readiness, you can start to gently and patiently make use of the following strategies:

- At first, just let your child get used to the potty chair. Let him sit on it fully clothed. Let him have a book or a toy to play with if he would like.

- Let your child see you using the toilet. Show him that his potty is just like your "big potty."

- Take your child to the potty when you are changing his diaper. Put the dirty diaper in the potty to show him what goes in there. If you trust him to not make a mess, you can even have him put the dirty diaper in the potty himself to give him a sense of control. This may go on for several weeks until he fully understands what the potty chair is for.

- Next, pay attention to how much time elapses between your child's bowel movements on average. Take your child to the potty at similar intervals and let her sit on it and try. Praise her for going with you and trying whether it results in a bowel movement or not.

- Pay attention to other signs that your child needs to use the potty. Chances are there will be certain facial expressions or behaviors that accompany the urge to eliminate. When you see these behaviors, you might say something like "It looks like your body is saying, 'time to use the potty!' Let's see." Then take your child to the potty chair. Whether or not anything happens, praise him for his willingness to listen to his body (and to you).

- We've mentioned it already, but the secret to successful potty training is praise, praise, and more praise.

Regardless of whether a particular encounter with potty time is productive, when your child is done, scoop her up in your arms, swing her around, and exclaim how *very* proud you are of her for trying to use the potty just like a big girl! Even do a little victory dance with your toddler in your arms. Try to get a giggle out of her. The goal is to make this time as loving and fun as possible—not so much with stickers or treats, but by drawing your child closer to you through affection and joy.

The process of potty training usually takes three to six months, although there may still be occasional accidents afterwards, and your child may have a hard time staying dry at night all the way through about age five. Just take it all in stride, be calm, praise your child's efforts (if you feel a little foolish you're probably doing it just about right), and trust that your child will eventually get there. Be patient with yourself and your child, and know that it will only be a matter of time before you take that last trip down the diaper aisle.

Final Thoughts on Discipline

In chapter 13, we state that the goal of discipline for toddlers is not compliance and consistent "good behavior." Rather, the goal of discipline at this age is teaching your child to be receptive; that is, showing your child both that you are the one who can help him reregulate when he is stressed, overwhelmed, or frustrated and that he can count on you to help him figure out what *to* do when he is gravitating toward things he ought *not* to do.

Consistent compliance and good behavior will not be the goal of discipline until your child is capable of at least basic self-regulation and self-control. These skills usually come with the development of internal self-talk between the ages of four and six. For now, you will continue to help your child learn to come to you for help calming down and deciding what to do instead. You will continue the three Rs of toddler discipline by repositioning or removing items that are too much of a temptation to avoid, redirecting your child toward activities he is allowed to do (instead of merely yelling at him to not do the things he is doing), and helping your child reregulate using time-in when he becomes frustrated or overwhelmed. This is really all there is to toddler discipline. Anything else is largely either overkill or completely ineffective at this age. Time-outs are mostly useless until age four to six, although you can use them in an extremely limited way to at least some effect on children as young as three; however, because children younger than three have such a limited attention span and so little ability to connect actions and consequences, they easily lose sight of why they have been put there. For practical advice on gentle, effective parenting for children three and up, check out our book *Parenting with Grace*.[1]

Hold On to the Magic

The biggest lesson we would like you to take away from this chapter is not to be afraid to hold on to your child's babyhood. Infancy and toddlerhood are really two phases of a single stage of childhood in which the primary goal is to help your child link his senses, brain, and muscles. In the first few months, you do this by attuning with your child to help her learn to set her basic body rhythms and develop the neural framework for processing the sensory input that is blasting her on all sides from the outside world. Next, you help her connect her brain up to her gross-motor muscles, which allow her to crawl, walk, and then run and explore. Finally, you help her brain interface with all her small-motor muscles so that she can begin to intentionally pick things up, move things where she wants them, and use the muscles of her mouth and tongue to form words and sentences. The whole process takes the entire first three years of life.

Too many parents think their child is—or at least should be—an independent almost-grown-up when he can run around, get into things, and form short sentences. However, these skills usher in the beginning of early childhood, not the end. For all intents and purposes, infancy extends throughout the first three years.

Again, we are certainly not encouraging you to hold your child back, coddle him, or emotionally smother him. By all means, let your child develop all the skills that he is capable of developing at every age and stage. Just be aware of what his brain and body are truly capable of and don't ever feel pressured—by yourself or others—to rush your baby through babyhood. Don't force independence on your child. Independence, by definition, must be taken, and your child will take it when he or she is ready. The first three years are a wonderful, magical time. Enjoy them to the fullest because, despite the fact that you will have many days that feel like they go on forever, when you look back on those first few years, you'll always wonder how they passed so quickly. Relish this time. Enjoy your baby. Celebrate the life you have brought into the world, and revel in your little one's dependence on you for as long as it lasts. Parents who do this raise strong children who are capable of standing on their own two feet when the time is right.

CHAPTER SEVENTEEN

When Is It Time for Your Next Baby?

Now that you're becoming a pro at the whole parenting-babies gig, you might start wondering when or whether it's time to reprise the role with another child. Many moms begin feeling especially wistful once their child leaves the cuddly baby stage and starts seeming a little more independent. Other parents feel like they are just beginning to climb out from under all the chaos and aren't quite ready to start again. How do you know when it's time to expand your family? How do you know what *God* wants?

Cookie Cutters Are for Baking

It is tempting to want cookie-cutter solutions to complex problems. Would that we could all turn to page xx in the catechism to find the answers to vexing questions like "Where *do* socks go when we put them in the dryer?," "Why *don't* men stop to ask for directions?," and "When *is* it time to have our next child?"

The Church herself tells us that there is no simple answer to this question. In the Second Vatican Council document *Gaudium et Spes,* the faithful are told that it is the couple's responsibility—and the couple's alone—to make the call "in the sight of God."[1]

So how do you know when it's time to take that next step? Here are a few tips to help you discern God's will for your family.

Live a Holy Life—Pray Regularly

Though he passed away a few years back, we were good friends with a very holy priest by the name of Fr. Ronald Lawler. In addition to being a profoundly faithful and dear man, he was an internationally renowned scholar and coeditor with then-Bishop Donald Wuerl of *The Teachings of Christ*. We once put the question of family size to him. "The first thing," he replied, "is to live a holy life."

His point was that making any decision "in the sight of God" first requires that we know how to hear God's voice and know his will. If a couple isn't striving together to live a holy life by praying together and discerning God's will about all the big and small decisions of daily life, then there is virtually no chance that they will ever be confident that they have found the "right answer"—that is, God's answer—to the question of how big their unique family should be. But the couple who regularly prays together and asks for God's guidance about daily problems, job situations, parenting questions, and other lesser issues, will have spirits well tuned to God's will and know that their hearts are ordered toward seeking God's plan for their family.

If you and your spouse aren't in the habit of praying regularly together about the practical decisions of everyday life, start today. If you don't know how to hear God speaking to you in prayer, then little books like *What Does God Want?* by Fr. Michael Scanlan and *Listening at Prayer* by Fr. Benedict Groeschel can be very helpful resources.

The next two points are important, but without having this first step in place, a family will always be tempted to try to turn general principles into a cookie-cutter recipe, or to look to others to tell them what to do, or to do what feels right regardless of what God's will might be. So, while you consider the following, first make sure that your prayer life is in order.

Consider the Family You Have

In *Gaudium et Spes*, the Church asks families to prayerfully consider the following when discerning whether it is time to have another child:

> Parents should regard as their proper mission the task of transmitting human life and educating those to whom it has been transmitted. . . . Let them thoughtfully take into account both their own welfare and that of their children, those already born and those which the future may bring. For this accounting they need to reckon with both the material and the spiritual conditions of the times as well as of their state in life. Finally, they should consult the interests of the family group, of temporal society, and of the Church herself.[2]

In other words, the Church asks families to consider that they need to *both* be open to the possibility of conceiving *and* be confident that they have what they need to teach their children to love God and to love each other. Regarding this latter point, when the Church says that parents are responsible for "educating" children, she doesn't just mean teaching them a trade or paying for college. The Church is referring to parents' obligation to teach children how to love God with all their heart, mind, soul, and strength and love their neighbor as themselves. That is tremendously wonderful and tremendously hard work. It takes a lot of energy. Catholics use the phrase *integral procreation* as a way of asserting that a child has the right not only to be conceived, but to be formed into a person who has been given everything he needs—not just in terms of knowledge, but also in terms of ability to love God and others and make good moral choices. Doing this requires a commitment to the kind of consistent presence, extravagant affection, and loving guidance we have been describing in this book. (For more on raising moral, loving children from infancy through young adulthood, see our book *Beyond the Birds and the Bees*).[3]

Some parents can provide this ongoing love, affection, and attention to both a baby and a toddler, and some just don't have the energy or the life circumstances to do so. Neither is right or wrong. Both conditions just *are*. You have to know whether you really have it in you to be fully present to each child, not just the next child. All of your children have a right to whatever they need from you at each stage of their development to become godly, moral people who love God and others with their whole heart, mind, and strength. Are you in a place where you feel reasonably certain that you have what it takes to give this to both your present child and the next one if you were to get pregnant at this time? If you feel, in prayer with your spouse, that the answer is "Yes, I think so," then that may be a good sign to move forward. If the answer is "I'm not sure" or "I don't think so," then you might need to pray and discern a little longer before deciding to have the next child.

Only the parents can know for sure whether or not their desire for another child (or lack thereof) is actually rooted in a genuine concern for—and an honest assessment of—the emotional, relational, and temporal resources they need to raise another saint for the kingdom.

Get Ready

The flip side, of course, is that some parents are so exhausted by the challenge of their first child that they have a hard time imagining having another child at any time. The Church genuinely sympathizes with you, and you must, of course, always defer to your honest assessment of your circumstances.

That said, your ongoing fertility is an invitation from God to at least continue praying about the question. Everything we write about listening to your body applies to you too. A couple should never find themselves saying "That's it. We're done." Rather, the couple should prayerfully ask, "If we don't try to have another child now, what do we need to do to acquire the additional emotional, relational, or temporal resources we believe are necessary to raise another saint for the kingdom?" By asking this question, the couple is able to approach objections to the possibility of another child both realistically and generously. For instance, it may be that parents decide that an older child's needs—or the couple's marital problems—require too much of their attention for them to be able to properly attend to a new baby at this time. But this should not be an excuse for never having more children. Rather, parents should say, "What can we do to overcome this child's behavior problems (or our marital struggles) so that we can free up the resources we need to raise another saint?" In this way, parents respect the call to unity/intimacy *and* the call to procreativity. When taking this approach, parents are able to remain open to life and to do so responsibly, keeping in mind not only their mission to be willing to have more children, but also their responsibility to raise those children in a faithful, loving environment that gives them the best education for living a holy life.

Work *with* Your Fertility

One qualifier we want to offer regarding the "listen to your body" concept is that some parents make the mistake of assuming that the return of fertility—which can happen as early as three weeks after birth (especially if you are not nursing) or be delayed as long as six months or more if you are nursing exclusively and on request—is God's way of saying "Okay! You're ready for the next one!" Nothing could be further from the truth. It might have been true if original sin had never entered into the world and the entire universe were still perfectly balanced and working exactly as God intended it to, but that is not the case. Because creation is clearly not always working in perfect harmony with God's plan, the return of fertility is merely an invitation to the couple to begin actively discerning, discussing, and praying to discover God's will for when they should have their next child. The point is that the return of fertility is just one important piece of information that you must take to prayer. You must also carefully consider the needs of the child you have, your needs, and the needs of your marriage and other circumstances, if you wish to truly live out the Church's call to responsible parenthood.

While discernment is hard work, it is a blessing to be able to be intentional about cooperating with God's plan for your family. If you are not aware of it, the Church gives couples another wonderful tool for helping them prayerfully discover God's plan for their fertility and their family. It is called *natural family planning (NFP)*. Independent studies show that NFP is as effective as other forms of family planning (more than 98 percent effective) for preventing pregnancy. It is also a terrific help in achieving pregnancy when the couple has discerned that they are ready for another child. Unlike artificial—and especially hormonal—birth control, NFP is perfectly healthy, does not pollute the environment, and is completely moral. One especially helpful method of natural family planning in the postpartum months is the Marquette Method, which uses an electronic fertility monitor to evaluate the levels of hormones in the woman's body that predict when she has begun ovulating again. (This can be tricky postpartum because the first ovulation occurs before menstruation.) Additionally, the Couple to Couple League (CCLI.org) offers both classes and personal, telephonic coaching to help couples more accurately predict the return of postpartum fertility. To learn more about how natural family planning can bless both your marriage and your discernment regarding God's plan for your family, check out our book *Holy Sex!: A Catholic Guide to Toe-Curling, Mind-Blowing, Infallible Loving.* [4]

Rejoice!

All discussion of discernment aside, we join the Church in heartily encouraging you to be as generous as you can when it comes to the question of having your next child. There is no greater gift than a baby. By all means, use whatever spacing you feel enables you to be as fully present to each of your children and your marriage as possible, but if God has placed another child on your heart, don't ever be afraid to take that leap at some point. We can't tell you the number of people we have met whose only regret is not having had more children. We have children from college age down to age seven, and we enjoy each one of them. When we look at our older children and see how much we enjoy their company and friendship, we feel so blessed that God gave us the courage to go ahead and bring them into the world even when we were scared or circumstances weren't perfect. In these times, we did as we're advising you now. We prayed and discerned, but we never hesitated to leap when we could reasonably be assured of meeting the needs of the children we had and attending to the needs of the next—and we're so glad we did! We know that you will be too. We believe in the importance of living life to the full as much as possible. Your children will help you to do this more than anything else you could ever take on. Relish the job of parenting. You will never be sorry you did.

CHAPTER EIGHTEEN

Help for the Journey

Thank you for allowing us to walk with you as you take your first steps toward becoming a Catholic family. What an exciting, incredible, exhausting, and rewarding time of life you are in!

When we look back on the sleepless nights, the diapers, the late-night feedings, and all the craziness that attends babyhood and toddlerhood, we can't help but smile. Was it hard? At times, of course it was. But was it worth it? You bet. We have done all the things we have recommended to you in this book and more, and it has paid off tremendously, not only for us, but for the thousands of parents who have followed our advice in *Parenting with Grace*, our radio program, and our counseling practice. It is our heartfelt desire that you should experience, with God's grace, the kind of joy and depth of closeness we celebrate in our family every single day. We hope that you are finding your parenting life as rewarding as we have and that you will continue to do so as the years go by.

Every family hits bumps in the road that they aren't sure they can handle. Building a family is on-the-job training, and even though we've shared much of what we've learned along the way, in addition to what research has to teach us all, there are many questions that just can't be answered adequately in a book. If you find yourself running up against questions you don't know how to answer or challenges you're not sure how to overcome in your parenting, personal, or marital life, we hope that you will consider us both your friends and a resource to help you along the way. There are several ways we can help.

First, be sure to tune in to our daily radio program, *More-2Life*, and call in with your questions. The show airs on over forty Catholic stations across the United States from noon to one o'clock Eastern, Monday through Friday. We would love to hear from you and help you more effectively apply all the information you have learned in this book and then some. Even if our show isn't carried on a radio station near you, feel free to tune in via our free iPhone or Android Ave Maria Radio apps. You can also post questions to us on our *More2Life Radio* Facebook page at www.facebook.com/More2LifeRadio.

Second, if you ever need more personal assistance, don't hesitate to contact us through the Pastoral Solutions Institute's tele-counseling practice. We understand how difficult it can be to sort through all the challenges to becoming the parent you'd like to be and having the family you want. If you are struggling and could use a friendly place to turn for advice, counsel, and new techniques or strategies for restoring order, peace, hope, and confidence to your heart, feel free to contact us through our website at www.CatholicCounselors.com or by calling 740-266-6461 to speak with a counselor.

Additionally, the following books, groups, and resources can be a great help in your present and future parenting work.

Books

Parenting with Grace: The Catholic Parent Guide to Raising (Almost) Perfect Kids by Dr. Greg and Lisa Popcak gives parents the tools they need to raise loving, godly children by creating a family around the principles found in St. John Paul II's Theology of the Body.

Beyond the Birds and the Bees: Raising Sexually Whole and Holy Kids by Dr. Greg and Lisa Popcak explores how to meet the challenge of raising moral kids in today's world. The book gives parents the tools they need to help children from toddlerhood to young adulthood exemplify the Catholic vision of life and love.

The Baby Book by Dr. Bill and Martha Sears is a comprehensive parenting resource addressing the common challenges of raising an infant and toddler.

The No-Cry Sleep Solution by Elizabeth Pantley is a great comfort to parents seeking a better night's sleep. It offers a wide variety of both parent-friendly and baby-friendly advice for tired moms and dads.

Other Resources

Pastoral Solutions Institute is an organization we founded that provides Catholic-integrated counseling services by telephone to couples, families, and individuals. Visit us at Catholic Counselors.com.

La Leche League International: Although now an international, secular organization supporting healthy nursing and attached parenting practices, this organization was founded by seven Catholic mothers and Dr. Herbert Ratner, the great Catholic physician, philosopher, educational reformer, and advisor to Pope Paul VI. The La Leche League is named for the Blessed Mother under the title La Sonora de La Leche (The Nursing Madonna). LLLI.org

Catholic Nursing Mother's League: An organization dedicated to promoting healthy nursing and the spirituality of parenting. CatholicBreastfeeding.org.

Attachment Parenting International: An organization dedicated to supporting parents, healthcare providers and educators with the tools they need to raise children to be loving people and responsible citizens. Dr. Popcak serves on the resource advisory council of API. See www.attachment parenting.org for more information.

Catholic Attachment Parenting Corner: A website dedicated to promoting the Seven Building Blocks of a Joyful Catholic Home. Also the home of *Tender Tidings*, a quarterly e-magazine of Catholic parenting and family life. www.CatholicAP.com

There is nothing more beautiful or more challenging than raising a faithful, loving family in today's world. We can't tell you what a blessing it is to know that there are parents like you who want to fulfill the Church's call to "build a civilization of love" by creating the kind of home that makes the angels smile. Sure, it's hard work, but together, we can help the world experience the truth behind the Catholic vision of love and family life.

When we first started out, we were terrified and excited, hopeful and intimidated all at the same time. We had no idea what a wonderful ride it would be, and we pray that you will find the grace to discover all the love that God has in store for your family. Don't ever be discouraged. God is with you, and we are here to help anytime you need it. We'd like to leave you with this last blessing based on Psalm 128:6 and Numbers 6:24–26:

> May you live to see your children's children.
> May God fill your home with his love.
> May the LORD bless your family and protect you always.
> May the LORD smile on your family and be gracious to you.
> May the LORD show you his favor and give you his peace,
> All the days of your life.
> Amen.

Notes

Chapter I: Getting Started

1. John Paul II, Angelus, March 25, 2001 (Vatican City: Libreria Editrice Vaticana, 2001), http://www.vatican.va/holy_father/john_paul_ii/angelus/2001/documents/hf_jp-ii_ang_20010325_en.html.

2. Francis, World Youth Day Welcome Ceremony Address, July 22, 2013 (Vatican City: Libreria Editrice Vaticana, 2013), http://www.vatican.va/holy_father/francesco/speeches/2013/july/documents/papa-francesco_20130722_gmg-cerimonia-benvenuto-rio_en.html.

3. Francis, Homily, October 27, 2013 (Vatican City: Libreria Editrice Vaticana, 2013), http://www.vatican.va/holy_father/francesco/homilies/2013/documents/papa-francesco_20131027_omelia-pellegrinaggio-famiglia_en.html.

4. Ibid.

5. John Paul II, *Evangelium Vitae* [The Gospel of Life], Encyclical on the Value and Inviolability of Human Life (Vatican City: Libreria Editrice Vaticana, 1995), 92, http://www.vatican.va/holy_father/john_paul_ii/encyclicals/documents/hf_jp-ii_enc_25031995_evangelium-vitae_en.html.

6. C. S. Lewis, *Mere Christianity* (San Francisco: HarperOne, 2009).

Chapter 2: Laying the Foundation

1. L. Cozolino, *The Neuroscience of Human Relationships* (New York: W. W. Norton, 2006).

2. D. Seigel, *The Pocket Guide to Interpersonal Neurobiology* (New York: W. W. Norton, 2012).

3. D. Seigel and M. Hartzell, *Parenting from the Inside Out* (New York: Tarcher, 2004).

4. G. Moran, L. Forbes, E. Evans, et al., "Both Maternal Sensitivity and Atypical Maternal Behavior Independently Predict Attachment Security and Disorganization in Adolescent Mother–Infant Relationships," *Infant Behavior and Development* 31, no. 2 (2008): 321–25; M. S. De Wollf and M. H. van Ijzendoom, "Sensitivity and Attachment: A Meta-Analysis on Parental Antecedents of Infant Attachment," *Child Development* 68, no. 4 (August 1997): 571–91; M. T. Owen and M. J. Cox, "Marital Conflict and the Development of Infant-Parent Attachment Relationships," *Journal of Family Psychology* 11, no. 2 (June 1997): 152–64.

5. Owen and Cox, "Marital Conflict," 152–64.

6. S. Guibert, "Modern Parenting May Hinder Brain Development, Research Shows," *Notre Dame News,* January 4, 2013, http://news.nd.edu/news/36653-modern-parenting-may-hinder-brain-development-research-shows/.

7. Paul VI, *Gaudium et Spes*: Pastoral Constitution on the Church in the Modern World (Vatican City: Libreria Editrice Vaticana, 1965), 24, http://www.vatican.va/archive/hist_councils/ii_vatican_council/documents/vat-ii_cons_19651207_gaudium-et-spes_en.html.

8. John Paul II, *Man and Woman He Created Them: A Theology of the Body*, trans. M. Waldstein (New York: Pauline, 2006).

Chapter 3: Routines and Rituals

1. B. Fiese, *Family Rituals and Routines.* (New Haven: Yale University Press, 2006).

Chapter 4: Getting to Know You!

1. John Paul II, *Man and Woman He Created Them*.

2. J. Maselko, L. Kubzansky, L. Lipsitt, and S. L. Buka, "Mother's Affection at 8 Months Predicts Emotional Distress in Adulthood," *Journal of Epidemiology and Community Health* 65, no. 7 (July 2010): 621–25.

3. Ibid.

4. W. Sears, M. Sears, J. Sears, and R. Sears, *The Baby Book: Everything You Need to Know about Your Baby from Birth to Age Two*, rev. ed. (New York: Little, Brown, 2013).

5. J. Marshall, "Infant Neurosensory Development: Considerations for Infant Child Care," *Journal of Early Childhood Education* 39 (2011): 175–81.

6. J. Wilkes, "Maternal Response to Infant Cries: An Analogue Study of Bidirectional Influences in Child Abuse," (dissertation, California School of Professional Psychology–San Diego, 1987), ProQuest, UMI Dissertations Publishing.

7. Cozolino, *Neuroscience of Human Relationships*; L. Thompson and W. Trevathan, "Cortisol Reactivity, Maternal Sensitivity, and Learning in 3-Month-Old Infants," *Infant Behavior and Development* 31, no. 1 (January 2008): 92–106.

8. S. Bell and M. Ainsworth, "Infant Crying and Maternal Responsiveness," *Child Development* 43, no. 4 (December 1972).

9. K. Tackett, Z. Cong, and T. Hale, "The Effect of Feeding Method on Sleep Duration, Maternal Well-Being, and Postpartum Depression," *Clinical Lactation* 2, no. 2 (2011): 22–26.

10. R. Lawrence, *Breastfeeding: A Guide for the Medical Professional*, 7th ed. (Maryland Heights, MO: Saunders Elsevier, 2010).

11. K. Pilyoung, R. Feldman, L. Mayes, et al., "Breastfeeding, Brain Activation to Own Infant Cry, and Maternal Sensitivity," *Journal of Child Psychology and Psychiatry* 52, no. 8 (2011): 907–15.

12. John Paul II, *Man and Woman He Created Them*.

13. Lawrence, *Breastfeeding*.

14. Ibid.

15. C. González, *My Child Won't Eat,* 2nd ed. (London: Pinter and Martin, 2012).

16. Lawrence, *Breastfeeding*.

17. Ibid.

18. D. Gibson, "Pope Francis Backs Public Breastfeeding! And That Makes Him Traditional . . . ," *Sacred and Profane Blog,* Religion News Service, December 17, 2013, http://davidgibson.religionnews.com/2013/12/17/pope-francis-backs-public-breastfeeding-makes-traditional/.

19. Lawrence, *Breastfeeding*; González, *My Child Won't Eat.*

20. J. Jansen, C. de Weerth, and J. M. Riksen-Walraven, "Breastfeeding and the Mother-Infant Relationship—A Review," *Developmental Review* 28, no. 4 (2008): 503–21.

21. J. Fowler, *Stages of Faith: The Psychology of Human Development and the Quest for Meaning* (San Francisco: HarperOne, 1995).

22. John Paul II, *Man and Woman He Created Them.*

23. Gibson, "Pope Francis Backs Public Breastfeeding!"

24. J. J. McKenna, *Sleeping with Your Baby: A Parent's Guide to Cosleeping* (Washington, DC: Platypus Media, 2007).

25. W. Sears, *Nighttime Parenting: How to Get Your Baby and Child to Sleep* (Schaumburg, IL: La Leche League International, 1999); McKenna, *Sleeping with Your Baby.*

26. P. Flemming, P. Blair, and J. McKenna, "Infant Death: New Knowledge, New Insights, and New Recommendations," *Archives of Diseases in Childhood* 16 (2006): 23–54.

27. C. Featherston and J. Leach, "Analysis of the Ethical Issues in the Breastfeeding and Bedsharing Debate," *Breastfeeding Review* 20, no. 3 (2012): 7–17.

28. Center for Injury Research and Policy, *Crib Safety* (Columbus, OH: Nationwide Children's Hospital, 2011), http://www.nationwidechildrens.org/cirp-cribs-playpens-and-bassinets.

29. John Paul II, *Man and Woman He Created Them.*

30. M. Sunderland, *The Science of Parenting* (New York: DK Adult, 2008).

31. Maselko et al., "Mother's Affection," 621–25.

32. J. Lyonfields, T. D. Borkovec, and J. Thayer, "Vagal Tone in Generalized Anxiety Disorder and the Effects of Aversive Imagery and Worrisome Thinking," *Behavior Therapy* 26, no. 3 (Summer 1995): 457–66; J. S. Chambers and J. J. Allen, "Vagal Tone as an Indicator of Treatment Response in Major Depression," *Psychophysiology* 39,

no. 6 (November 2002): 861–64; J. Rash and A. Aguirre-Camacho, "Attention Deficit Hyperactivity Disorder and Cardiac Vagal Tone: A Systematic Review," *ADHD Attention Deficit and Hyperactivity Disorders* 4, no. 4 (2012).

33. W. Middlemiss, D. Granger, W. Goldberg, and L. Nathans, "Asynchrony of Mother-Infant Hypothalamic-Pituitary-Adrenal Axis Activity Following Extinction of Infant Crying Responses Induced during the Transition to Sleep," *Early Human Development* 88, no. 4 (April 2012): 227–32.

34. A. Price, M. Wake, and O. C. Ukoumunne, "Five-Year Follow-Up of Harms and Benefits of Behavioral Infant Sleep Intervention: Randomized Trial," *Pediatrics* 130, no. 4 (October 2012): 643–51.

35. G. Belenky, N. Wesensten, D. Thorne, et al., "Patterns of Performance Degradation and Restoration during Sleep Restriction and Subsequent Recovery: A Sleep Dose-Response Study," *Journal of Sleep Research* 12, no. 1 (2003): 1–12.

36. J. Edinger and M. K. Means, "Cognitive-Behavioral Therapy for Primary Insomnia," *Clinical Psychological Review* 25, no. 5 (2005): 539–58.

37. G. Esposito, S. Yoshida, O. Ryuko, et al., "Infant Calming Responses during Maternal Carrying in Humans and Mice," *Current Biology* 23, no. 9 (2013): 739–45.

Chapter 5: Keeping Mama Happy

1. J. Paulson, D. Sharnail, and M. S. Bazemore, "Prenatal and Postpartum Depression in Fathers and Its Association with Maternal Depression: A Meta-Analysis," *Journal of the American Medical Association* 303, no. 19 (2010): 1961–69, doi:10.1001/jama.2010.605.

2. E. Robertson, S. Grace, T. Wallington, and D. Stewart, "Antenatal Risk Factors for Post Partum Depression: A Synthesis of Recent Literature," *General Hospital Psychiatry* 26 (2004): 289–95; C. Lee and W. Doherty, "Marital Satisfaction and Father Involvement during the Transition to Parenthood," *Fathering: A Journal of Theory, Research and Practice* 5, no. 2 (2007).

3. B. Mossop, "The Brains of Our Fathers: Does Parenting Rewire Dads?," *Scientific American*, August 17, 2010, http://www.scientificamerican.com/article/the-brains-of-our-fathers/.

4. L. Gettler, T. W. McDade, A. B. Feranil, and C. W. Kuzawa, "Longitudinal Evidence That Fatherhood Decreases Testosterone in Human Males," Proceedings of the National Academy of Sciences 10.1073 (2011); L. Gettler, J. McKenna, T. W. McDade, et al., "Does Cosleeping Contribute to Lower Testosterone Levels in Fathers? Evidence from the Philippines," *PLOSone* 10.1371 (2012).

5. John Paul II, *Man and Woman He Created Them.*

6. Lawrence, *Breastfeeding.*

7. Northwestern University, "Postpartum Depression: Surprising Rate of Women Depressed after Baby," ScienceDaily, March 14, 2013, http://www.sciencedaily.com/releases/2013/03/130314124618.htm.

Chapter 6: Growing Closer

1. John Paul II, *Familiaris Consortio,* Apostolic Exhortation on the Role of the Christian Family in the Modern World (Vatican City: Libreria Editrice Vaticana, 1981), 21, http://www.vatican.va/holy_father/john_paul_ii/apost_exhortations/documents/hf_jp-ii_exh_19811122_familiaris-consortio_en.html.

2. University of Denver, "Children Take a Toll on Marital Bliss," ScienceDaily, April 8, 2009, http://www.sciencedaily.com/releases/2009/04/090408145351.htm.

3. Springer, "Married with Children the Key to Happiness?," ScienceDaily, October 27, 2009, http://www.sciencedaily.com/releases/2009/10/091027101420.htm.

4. G. K. Popcak and L. Popcak, *Just Married: The Catholic Guide to Surviving and Thriving in the First Five Years of Marriage* (Notre Dame, IN: Ave Maria, 2013).

5. G. K. Popcak, *Holy Sex! A Catholic Guide to Mind-Blowing, Toe-Curling, Infallible Loving* (New York: Crossroad, 2008).

Chapter 7: The Spiritual Life of Your Newborn

1. Fowler, *Stages of Faith.*

2. A. Hart, J. Limke, and P. Budd, "Attachment and Faith Development," *Journal of Psychology and Theology* 38, no. 2 (2010): 122–28.

3. D. Narvaez and D. K. Lapsley, *Personality, Identity, and Character: Explorations in Moral Psychology* (New York: Cambridge University Press, 2009).

4. Cozolino, *Neuroscience of Human Relationships*.

5. Maselko et al., "Mother's Affection," 621–25.

6. G. K. Popcak and L. Popcak, *Beyond the Birds and the Bees: Raising Sexually Whole and Holy Kids* (West Chester, PA: Ascension, 2012).

7. Seigel, *Pocket Guide to Interpersonal Neurobiology*.

8. *The Catechism of the Catholic Church*, 2nd ed. (Washington: United States Catholic Conference, 2000), http://www.usccb.org/beliefs-and-teachings/what-we-believe/catechism/catechism-of-the-catholic-church/epub/index.cfm.

9. Ibid.

10. J. Alter, "The Power of Names," *New Yorker*, June 2013; J. M. Tierney, "A Boy Named Sue and a Theory of Names," *New York Times*, March 11, 2008.

Chapter 8: Time to Get Moving

1. Lawrence, *Breastfeeding*.

2. B. Gibbs and R. Forste, "Breastfeeding, Parenting, and Early Cognitive Development," *Journal of Pediatrics* 164, no. 3 (2014).

3. Sears et al., *Baby Book*.

Chapter 9: Attack of the Shoulds

1. C. Wooden, "Marriage Isn't Always Easy, but It's Beautiful," Catholic News Service, October 25, 2013, http://www.catholicnews.com/data/stories/cns/1304506.htm.

Chapter 10: Work-Life Balance

1. K. P. Erb, "Study Shows That Numbers of Working Moms Have Increased: Is That a Good Thing?," *Forbes*, May 31, 2013, http://www.forbes.com/sites/kellyphillipserb/2013/05/31/study-shows-that-numbers-of-working-moms-have-increased-is-that-a-good-thing/.

2. National Institute of Child Health and Human Development, *Study of Early Child Care and Youth Development* (Bethesda, MD: US Department of Health and Human Services, National Institute of Health, 2012), http://www.nichd.nih.gov/research/supported/Pages/seccyd.aspx.

3. *CCC*, 2426–36.

4. John Paul II, *Evangelium Vitae*, 92.

5. Wooden, "Marriage Isn't Always Easy."

Chapter 12: Supporting Your Little Explorer

1. Lawrence, *Breastfeeding*.

2. American Academy of Pediatrics, "Breastfeeding and the Use of Human Milk"—Section on Breastfeeding, *Pediatrics* 115, no. 2 (2005): 496–506; 2004–2491.

3. Mayo Clinic, "Extended Breastfeeding: What You Need to Know," accessed December 2, 2013, http://www.mayoclinic.com/health/extended-breastfeeding/MY02128; Lawrence, *Breastfeeding*.

4. World Health Organization, "Infant and Young Child Feeding," accessed December 2, 2013, http://www.who.int/mediacentre/factsheets/fs342/en/index.html.

5. M. F. Small, *Our Babies, Ourselves: How Biology and Culture Shape the Way We Parent* (New York: Anchor Books, 1999).

6. E. Pantley, *The No-Cry Sleep Solution for Toddlers and Preschoolers* (New York: McGraw-Hill, 2005).

Chapter 13: Healthy Toddler Discipline

1. Popcak and Popcak, *Beyond the Birds and the Bees*.

2. A. Kazdin, *The Kazdin Method for Parenting the Defiant Child*, (Boston: Mariner Books, 2009).

3. J. Chrysostom, *An Address on Vainglory and the Right Way Parents Should Bring Up Their Children*, http://www.strobertbellarmine.net/books/Chrysostom--Vainglory_and_Children.pdf.

4. J. B. de la Salle, *On the Conduct of Christian Schools*, http://www.lasallian.info/doc/Conduct%20-%202007%20reprint.pdf.

5. J. Bosco, *The Preventive System,* http://www.salesians.org/pastoral.html.

6. Sunderland, *Science of Parenting.*

7. G. K. Popcak and L. Popcak, *Parenting with Grace: The Catholic Parents' Guide to Raising (Almost) Perfect Kids* (Huntington, IN: Our Sunday Visitor, 2010).

Chapter 14: Turning the Corner

1. American Academy of Pediatrics, "Media Use by Children Younger than 2 Years," American Academy of Pediatrics Council on Communications and Media Executive Committee, *Pediatrics* 128, no. 5 (2011).

2. B. Carey, "Parents Urged Again to Limit TV for Youngest," *New York Times,* October 18, 2011, http://www.nytimes.com/2011/10/19/health/19babies.html?_r=0.

3. Ben Worthen, "The Perils of Texting while Parenting," WSJ.com, September 30, 2012, http://online.wsj.com/news/articles/SB10000872396390444772404577589683644202996.

Chapter 15: Spiritual Care of the Toddler

1. United States Conference of Catholic Bishops, "Call to Family, Community, and Participation," accessed December 2, 2013, http://www.usccb.org/beliefs-and-teachings/what-we-believe/catholic-social-teaching/call-to-family-community-and-participation.cfm.

2. Elfie Hinterkopf, *Integrating Spirituality in Counseling: A Manual for Using the Experiential Focusing Method* (Ross-on-Wye, UK: PCCS Books, 2008).

3. Paul VI, *Lumen Gentium,* Dogmatic Constitution on the Church (Vatican City: Libreria Editrice Vaticana, 1964), 11, http://www.vatican.va/archive/hist_councils/ii_vatican_council/documents/vat-ii_const_19641121_lumen-gentium_en.html.

Chapter 16: Enjoying the Terrific Twos

1. Popcak and Popcak, *Parenting with Grace.*

Chapter 17: When Is It Time for Your Next Baby?

1. Paul VI, *Gaudium et Spes*, 50.

2. Ibid.

3. Popcak and Popcak, *Beyond the Birds and the Bees*.

4. Popcak, *Holy Sex!*

ALSO BY DR. GREG AND LISA POPCAK

Marriage and Sexuality

Just Married
Holy Sex!
For Better . . . FOREVER!
The Exceptional Seven Percent

Parenting and Family

Beyond the Birds and the Bees
Parenting with Grace

Faith and Life

God Help Me! These People Are Driving Me Nuts!
God Help Me! This Stress Is Driving Me Crazy!
The Life God Wants You to Have

Programs

Living A Joy-Filled Marriage
A Marriage Made for Heaven

Gregory K. Popcak is executive director of Pastoral Solutions Institute and the author of more than twenty popular books and programs integrating Catholic theology and counseling psychology. He is an expert on the practical applications of the theology of the body. Popcak's books include *Just Married*, *Holy Sex!*, and *Parenting with Grace*. He is a regular contributor to *Catholic Digest*, *Family Foundations*, and other magazines.

Since 2001, he and his wife and coauthor, Lisa Popcak, have hosted several nationally syndicated radio advice programs, including *Heart, Mind and Strength; Fully Alive!* and, most recently, *More2Life*. They have also hosted two television series for EWTN: *For Better . . . FOREVER!* and *God Help Me!* Popcak serves as an adjunct professor for the sociology and graduate theology departments at the Franciscan University of Steubenville. He also serves as adjunct faculty for the Harold Abel School of Social and Behavioral Health at Capella University.

Lisa Popcak is vice president of the Pastoral Solutions Institute, a family-life coach, lactation consultant, and a professional educator. She is the coauthor of *Just Married*, and *Parenting with Grace*. Since 2001, she and her husband and coauthor, Gregory Popcak, have hosted several nationally syndicated radio advice programs, including *Heart, Mind and Strength; Fully Alive!* and, most recently, *More2Life*. They have also hosted two television series for EWTN: *For Better . . . FOREVER!* and *God Help Me!*

Lisa Popcak's articles can be read in many popular Catholic magazines. A sought-after speaker on marriage, parenting, and women's spirituality, she has addressed audiences across North America as well as in Australia and Hong Kong.

Founded in 1865, Ave Maria Press,
a ministry of the Congregation of
Holy Cross, is a Catholic publishing
company that serves the spiritual and
formative needs of the Church and its
schools, institutions, and ministers;
Christian individuals and families; and
others seeking spiritual nourishment.

For a complete listing of titles from

Ave Maria Press

Sorin Books

Forest of Peace

Christian Classics

visit www.avemariapress.com

 ave maria press® / Notre Dame, IN 46556
A Ministry of the United States Province of Holy Cross